Dancing Through the Digital Revolution

A MARKETING PLAYBOOK

BY DANIEL FLAMBERG

Dancing Through the Digital Revolution

ISBN: 978-0-9979654-1-4

Library of Congress Control number: 2017938056

Published by:
Simply Good Press
www.simplygoodpress.com
Montclair, NJ USA

Cover Design: Whitney Pillsbury

For Fern

The renowned broadcast journalist, Edward R. Murrow, said, "Anyone who isn't confused really doesn't understand the situation." The marketing and media industry is like that; a confusing mess of, sometimes contradictory, trends, concepts, technologies, and players.

In *'Dancing through the Digital Revolution*: a marketing playbook,' Daniel Flamberg provides a guiding light into this confusing industry. From Big Data to Omnichannel Strategy and Mobile Coupons, Mr. Flamberg provides valuable insights and advice. He cuts through vague terms and marketing hype, which will help both newcomers and seasoned veterans in the marketing and media industry find clarity and understanding.

Matthew Sawyer, Adjunct Professor at Columbia University, teaches a graduate course called "The Evolving Industry" in the Masters of Strategic Communication Program

Danny Flamberg has an uncanny ability to take the complex and confusing and synthesize and simplify it for easy and practical application. Whether you are struggling to make sense of the ever-changing digital/social/mobile maelstrom or are a true native, this book is a great "go-to" to getting it right."

Robin Koval, CEO Truth Initiative

"I've known Daniel for ages and he's one of the sharpest minds in the world of digital marketing. He definitely has danced a variety of styles through the world of marketing over the past two decades. Most of what he says is based on tests that help obliterate bias that usually plagues the industry and the false gurus and prophets that inhabit it. Danny notes how engagement is a terrible metric and I tend to agree. This is an unpopular point of view, but when you read this book, that's the section that will be the most useful. It will prepare you to not only dance, but to improvise, which can help you navigate the noisy digital revolution."

Geoffrey Colon, Communications Designer at Microsoft and author of *Disruptive Marketing: What Growth Hackers, Data Punks, And Other Hybrid Thinkers Can Teach Us About Navigating the New Normal*.

'Dancing through the digital revolution' is like nothing else you've read on how to transform cultures through digital media. True to the title, Danny Flamberg offers clear step-by-step instructions on how to help your company adapt to the digital revolution quickly and gracefully — and better than anyone else in your field.

From strategies to overcome organizations' cultural norms and barriers, to improving e-mail open and click rates, Danny Flamberg brings his considerable wit and wisdom to helping you and your company be winners in the digital revolution that's transforming the way we do business.

Johanna Skilling, Head of Planning, Ogilvy CommonHealth

I read a good deal - it's basically all I do - but Danny's writing has a way of keeping me engaged in a way that most business writers do not. It's rare to come across a book that is equal parts practical, actionable, and captivating, but that's exactly how I'd describe *'Dancing through the digital revolution'*. If you're even remotely concerned with falling behind the competition, this is the book you need to be reading.

Jeremy Goldman, The Firebrand Group

From awareness to engagement and advocacy, from broadcast advertising to omnichannel, from human relationships to Big Data, ...

Danny delivers the understanding of the essential routes to market any business needs to consider when being successful in digital marketing today and tomorrow. His thoughts and advice are compelling one-pagers, stimulating reflections of strategy and execution.

Raimund Mollenhauer, Co-Founder of SAP Community and Digital Marketing Entrepreneur

"Danny Flamberg has been a key member of my select 'inner circle' of marketing thought leaders for the past two decades. A superb writer, he uses piercing intellect and vivid storytelling to splinter the gushing fire hose of modern marketing into small streams of valuable and actionable insight. *'Dancing through the Digital Revolution'* will help you take the right steps in your digital marketing journey."

Jerry Bernhart, Principal, Bernhart Associates Executive Search, LLC.

"This is essential reading for anyone who uses digital media in their business or in their personal lives. Danny Flamberg is one of America's most respected practitioners of digital communications, whether it is CRM, email or digital content of any kind.

Reading this will put digital communications into clear focus. It is practical and must be read. While I am in this field every day, it actually gave me new perspective and new ideas. Anyone who reads this will be the better for it."

Paul S. Gumbinner, President, The Gumbinner Company, Inc.

"I've known Daniel Flamberg for a long time and I continue to be amazed by him.

When we first met, a number of years ago, I worked in an ad agency in Brazil and Danny handled RAB - Radio Advertising Bureau`s Marketing.

We became friends and I continued to follow his career. Danny focused on the market dynamics, the communication channels, the customers, and the audience. He always came back with a new idea, another way of seeing the problems and then creating the solutions.

In reading Dancing Through the Digital Revolution, it is incredible how we can see the recent history of communication developing, the consumer or the audience getting stronger, and always through the vision of Danny that, fortunately, shows us that there are no ready-made formulas, that the human being is unique, that we are smarter and more complex than, sometimes, people try to convince us.

For me, this ability to see the other side of things, the less obvious questions, always presented in a humorous way, is why I have the greatest admiration for Danny Flamberg."

Geraldo Leite, Singular Media & Conteúdo

CONTENTS

FOREWORD BY LINDA KAPLAN THALER

The digital revolution disrupted the theory and the practice of marketing and advertising in ways big and small. Very few among us could anticipate or envision the wide ranging and continuously changing impact of the Internet, search, interactivity, mobility and social media on how we frame and communicate commercial messages to customers and prospects.

One of the people who saw the revolution coming, understood how it would change things and knew how to selectively use it, integrate it and explain it to others is Danny Flamberg, who has been my digital Sherpa for many years. A gifted and practical marketer, with both academic and experiential pedigrees, he has been a digital strategy innovator, evangelist and go-to-guy for leading brands, insurgent competitors and promising start-ups for the last twenty years. Practical and results-oriented with the ability to come up with a big idea, he is unfazed by the latest shiny object. He has the rare ability to make complex and complicated information accessible, easy and fun.

Schooled in the newest technology but skeptical about the latest and greatest claims, Danny can pick and choose the right tools to reach and persuade the right audiences at the right time and in the right channel. He has the perspective, knows the context and has the experience to separate genuine innovations from the hype and to connect new ideas and approaches to proven theories and practices.

His essays in this book reflect a hard-headed, goal-oriented approach to using new technology and new channels in service to classical marketing objectives. Pointed, critical and often funny, his observations on the strategy and tactics underlying the use and adoption of emerging technologies help marketers connect the dots, see the creative, media and relationship possibilities and plan sensible cost effective marketing and advertising campaigns.

Dancing Through the Digital Revolution is a playbook for marketing and advertising professionals. The insights are distinctive and well researched, the technology has been vetted in real life situations and the advice is rooted in operational experience and best practices. Reading these essays will give you a basic grounding in current marketing practice and technology as well as proven, sometimes step-by-step, directions to deploy and use digital assets, Big Data, marketing technology, relationship marketing, mobile devices and social networks effectively.

– Linda Kaplan Thaler, Former Chairman of Publicis Kaplan Thaler, best-selling author, speaker, and member of the Advertising Hall of Fame, March 2017

INTRODUCTION: PERSPECTIVES

Change Management Lessons from Chairman Mao

If you are trying to change an organization's culture, you cannot ignore the transformation of the People's Republic of China under Mao Zedong.

And while Chairman Mao and his successors' philosophy, approach and policies are abhorrent in so many ways, the Chinese Communist Party (CCP) brought China into the modern world. How they did it offers lessons in change management that can be applied in more benign environments.

Involve Top Leadership. Every Chinese leader has been an active front man and spokesperson for change. Routine and regular appearances to underscore the effort and tout the party line are key expectations of top leaders.

Create a Party Line. The CCP plans their work and works their plan. They articulate a clear, concise policy line and demand active adherence. The existence of a clear point of view and clearly articulated short and long-term goals direct and orient the organization.

Use Simple Slogans Frequently. While the CCP will never win any creative awards, they understood early on that communicating big concepts required shorthand that is universally and instantly understood and frequently repeated. Short punchy slogans bombarded the masses until they were unavoidable, unforgettable and firmly drilled into everyone's consciousness.

Influence Every Unit. By identifying early adopters and designating change leaders at each level of society, the CCP mobilized and motivated millions of "change agents" to accomplish their mission. Every house, block, factory, military unit and sector of society had party members and trained cadres tasked with instigating and sustaining change. Change requires worker bees at every important level of the organization.

Model Behavior. People need to understand what is expected of them. By calling out model citizens, model work brigades and model collective farms, the CCP held up the desired behavior and then dissected and disseminated the operative elements of the behavior they sought to encourage. By showing the end result, often entirely fabricated, they drove behavioral change by showing the path forward step-by-step, focusing on the desired end result.

Celebrate Every Victory. The corollary to modeling behavior is celebrating every win. In the case of the CCP many victories were entirely bogus. Nonetheless, they understood that change is an incremental process where success builds upon itself. Small victories can be compounded, packaged and merchandized to yield increasingly bigger victories. They also understood the need for people to join a winning team and the attractiveness of perceived momentum as a recruiting and validating device.

Marshal Peer Pressure. People do what others are doing and often comply with widely held expectations. We live in monkey-see, monkey-do cultures. The CCP used every form of peer pressure and coercion to attain conformity. Their methods, while odious and brutal, built a culture where the community reinforced and policed its own behavior. This was further reinforced by the use of content and tangible experiences, music, operas and common symbols (e.g. The Little Red Book, Mao pins) to consistently reinforce the message. Accepting and implementing change is a viral process that builds on itself until it reaches critical mass.

Focus on Self-Interest. The CCP aggressively used the "performance review process" backed by secret police and Gestapo tactics to help people act in their own best interests. Backing expected behavior into key performance indicators, affecting compensation and into personal objectives, yields uptake and traction.

Provide a Feedback Loop. Genuine attitudinal change is incremental and evolutionary. By creating ways to solicit ideas, participation and express dissent or frustration, the party kept the effort on track, adapted the plan to changing circumstances, accounted for anomalies and absorbed the best ideas for moving forward, often over the dead bodies of dissenters.

Historians will debate the legacy of Chairman Mao forever, arguably the greatest cynical tyrant and mass murderer of all time. But the average Chinese person today enjoys a quality of life unimaginable just 70 years ago. Within this massive sustained transformation, with all its flaws, evil and inconsistencies, are lessons in change management worthy of observing and extracting.

Trump's Marketing Lessons

Love him or hate him, Donald Trump is an outstanding instinctive marketer. His campaign offers eight lessons in marketing and communications strategy; some troubling, others innovative.

Create a Character. Big, brash, loud, ugly, crass with a comb-over, "The Donald" created a persona—the strongman—that was consistent throughout the campaign. He set himself up as an outsider with the unique ability to assess and critique everything and everyone. He repeatedly and consistently claimed business expertise, practical wisdom and common sense regardless of the facts.

Flout Convention. Trump broke the mold for Presidential candidates. Courtesy, consideration, thoughtfulness and decorum were ignored in favor of ego, bombast and insults. Deviating from the norm drew spectacular unearned media attention and regularly hijacked media cycles. Trump was not concerned with being polarizing.

In fact, he consciously created OMG and WTF moments. Playing the gruff outsider untainted by political or military experience energized his core supporters who evidently ignored repeated accusations against him and some obvious facts. Trump routinely surprised and flanked his competitors with one outrage after another, using tactics they wouldn't follow and couldn't stomach or counter.

Know Your Audience. Trump grasped and channeled the repressed anger and frustration alive throughout the country. Ironically, a billionaire positioned himself as the champion of the people. He rallied demographic groups at the other end of the economic spectrum and offered an alternative to two clueless parties who failed to understand, anticipate or respond to their primary constituency.

Keep it Simple. Trump's wall, tax cuts, bad trade deals, claims of a rigged election and opposition to Obamacare were clear, unambiguous tent pole ideas. Slogans and catch phrases trumped nuance and subtlety. Everyone knew where Trump stood, regardless of his or her appreciation for his point of view. His secret plan to take down ISIS and "Make America Great Again" stood in contrast to the more carefully phrased and heavily calculated positions of his opponents.

Label the Competition. "Crooked Hillary," "Little Marco," "low energy Jeb," Lindsey Graham the "idiot" and "Lyin' Ted" positioned and poisoned the competitors and sowed fear, uncertainty and doubt among voters. Trump carved out a positioning and sidetracked the policy conversation by demeaning others. His competitors were defined by Trump rather than by their own proactive marketing.

Tell the Big Lie. Unfortunately, this age-old propaganda technique still works. Tell a whopper. Repeat it incessantly as loud as possible. Reinforce it with adjectives like "disaster," "disgraceful," "disgusting" or "criminal" and sway a majority.

Frequency Counts. Say it loud. And say it over and over. Ignore facts, criticism or correction. The constant repetition of themes, insults and charges, regardless of their veracity, established a tone and an agenda for the campaign. Slogans and chants in simple language created a point of connection, affinity and identification for angry voters.

Own a Channel. Trump's virtual takeover of Twitter gave him a distinct voice and a real-time vehicle to incite, insult and respond. His mastery of the channel and in timing his tweets forced media to cover him and forced other candidates to embrace his channel in defense and communicate on his terms.

Trump differentiated his brand, resonated with his target audiences, grabbed disproportionate media coverage and forever changed the complexion of public discourse. Some of his tactics are applicable to brands seeking a competitive edge.

Instigating Innovation

Innovation is our highest aspiration and our most meaningless buzzword. The quest for a new idea, device, method or process of introducing new ideas, devices or methods animates the C suite. Nobody wants to be ancient, hidebound or left behind. Everyone aspires to be innovative.

Companies are hiring innovation gurus, empaneling task forces and opening innovation labs or centers of excellence at a breakneck pace to keep up with cultural and technological change and to convince themselves that they have a clue about what's going to happen next. The intention is to overcome the iron law of bureaucracy and the inevitability of silos by being agile and nimble in chaotic and competitive marketplaces.

Innovation is partly about attitude and partly about finding disruptive processes and products to get ahead faster. It's about thinking about and doing things differently. With an assumption, often unarticulated, that innovation has to be infused or ingested into an organization rather than grown organically, leaders are scrambling to find catalysts to move faster, better and smarter.

There is a healthy unresolved debate about how much inside knowledge is necessary to innovate. Some argue you must understand the internal mechanisms and dynamics of an industry or a business to effectively re-engineer it. Others argue that kicking over the checkerboard is sufficient. Inside insights actually impede innovation rather than fuel it. There are cases to support both points of view.

There is a parallel debate about how innovation takes root or doesn't. Some argue training advocates, redesigning processes and imposing top-down mandates, can graft innovation into an existing organization. Others argue that without widespread and repetitive training, incentives, enforcement and genuine employee engagement and acceptance you cannot teach an old dog new tricks. Here, too, there are cases documenting either point of view

Here is a quick tour of the leading tactics in the race to innovate American business.

Import Gurus. There is no shortage of speakers, experts and consultants selling organizational change and innovation. It's a Baskin Robbins of blab. Transformation is on everyone's lips. There are endless ideas and inspirations to be had. But there are fewer nuts and bolts formulas to get from today to a better place.

Create Innovation Teams. Many business put together diverse multi-disciplinary teams with complementary skill sets and functional or geographic representation to puzzle out the innovation problem. Set outside the bounds of day-to-day business, these insiders generally know what's working and what's not. But getting to what will work better is rarely a lay-up. In order to have any effect, these teams need C level sponsorship, a well-defined mandate, a timetable and specific instructions on deliverables. Otherwise it becomes a frustrated debating society.

Staff a B Team. Taking a page from government, some firms have put together cross-functional teams and charged them with simulating tough competitors. Asking savvy insiders to blow up the existing business, find competitive weaknesses or apply disruptive technologies can ideally yield a roadmap for innovation, which could pre-empt competitive inroads and/or turn vulnerabilities into competitive advantages. Asking some of the best players to take down your business requires a willingness to listen to and accept their insights and recommendations.

Hire Outsiders. Using consultants or hiring outsiders is a classic tactic for bringing new perspective into an organization. Often senior level hires bring vastly different points of view, experiences and staff with them, which can transform policies and procedures. The same holds true for consulting firms who frequently have a broad and deep perspective on the competitors and the business dynamics among competitors. Though, in some cases, what worked in Company A won't work in Company B.

Hire Newbies. Fresh ideas come from the mouths of babes is the philosophy behind this tactic. Hire millennials who are digital natives and who are your next best customers. Ask them to reinvent your business. Free from being part of an existing company or organizational culture, they start with a blank slate to reimagine products, services and engagement the way they'd want it. And while you might have to filter their ideas for practicality, timing or cost, you might gain a completely new approach or a leg up on the competition.

Align with Start-ups and Accelerators. Invest in or align with people creating new forms of business and import their best findings is the cornerstone of this approach. Isolated from the dynamics of the main business, watch, learn and cherry pick the best ideas and the best people from businesses at earlier stages of formation. To some extent this harvests the best IP and the newest insights or applications of technology from the vast majority of new companies that fail.

Nobody has cracked the innovation code. And nobody has a corner on the market for rapid improvements or new ideas. Intention and openness drive investments of time, resources and money in innovation projects. Leadership and competitive necessity separate out the real innovators and drive adoption of innovative policies, practices, products or procedures.

SECTION I

STRATEGIES/ CHANNELS / TACTICS

Developing an Omnichannel Strategy

The quest for an omnichannel ad strategy is about the evolution of storytelling. The latest buzzword, taking root among the digerati, is nothing more than a cry for direction in how to frame, parse and deliver a brand's story to audiences most likely to embrace it.

The search for a new storytelling paradigm is part of the evolution of advertising from an awareness medium to an engagement medium. As channels and devices proliferate and classic brand loyalty ebbs, it's harder and harder to find, reach, motivate and persuade people. Add mobility and the functionality to connect and share in real time across geographies and you find your target audience infinitely more elusive.

People don't think or act in a straight line. They use a variety of media and devices in millions of idiosyncratic ways to learn about brands and make purchases. The sequence of action and the cumulative effect or the reinforcing factors of messaging are logical to assume, but impossible to measure accurately. We know our customers use these channels and seek out an array of media. We're not sure how or when to engage them emotionally, intellectually or cost effectively with our product or brand story, although we suspect there is a sequence or a formula to achieve optimum attention, consideration and preference.

This suspicion is driving the search for an omnichannel strategy that can be measured and proven to work. Generally, organic and paid search form the baseline for most communications campaigns. Like a musical baseline, they define the terms and establish a rhythm mirroring the first expression of attention or interest by consumers. But search might be the only consensus vehicle.

Two principal creative approaches seem to be in perennial test.

One Voice. Put the same message everywhere. This surround-sound or matching luggage strategy is classic for new product or service introductions or to hammer home a new or improved selling point. It gives brands a way to generate significant reach, frequency and memorability quickly, and to engage customers and prospects with a one-size-fits-all message. It trades awareness for nuances and segments, but can give a brand significant attention for as long as the campaign is sustained.

Parse the Messages. Make assumptions about the role and relative persuasive impact of each channel and device and craft creative content so that the sum of the parts is equal to or greater than the whole. Put your heavy product description on the website and bring it to life or animate it on YouTube. Drive traffic with related messages in search, display and email. Bolster the concept, solicit consumer reaction, input and reviews and expose the back story in social and mobile media and assume that customers and prospects will use some combination of channels to get the key ideas in your campaign. Put features and benefits in some channels and offers or incentives in others. Link the pieces and parts as best as you can and hope for and measure the result.

The proliferation of channels and devices, 24/7/365 communications, and usage patterns by segment that are equally hard to identify, predict, monitor and measure demand creative testing to get to an optimal omnichannel strategy.

Managing Multichannel Marketing

Multichannel marketers want the whole enchilada: a multichannel, multi-dimensional, multi-faceted, efficiently budgeted marketing program, wrapped up in a ROI-positive bow.

The ultimate challenge and fantasy is to find a way to synchronize target psycho-demographics with a detailed customer journey that integrates with a brand's posture, positioning, content and channel ecosystem. While at the same time it aligns with a comprehensive media budget executed using the latest and greatest technology in service to measurable business goals. And extra credit if this tall order fits on a single slide.

But there are eight significant speed bumps that must be overcome on the road to nirvana.

No Silver Bullet. There is no universal formula for mastering multichannel marketing. There may be repeatable and scalable tactics for individual brands or brand portfolios, but the number of independent and contingent variables make a universal MCM plan impossible.

Customer Experience is the Driver. Start by defining whom you need to speak with and what you want those people to see, hear, think, feel and do. The answer to these questions is rarely automatic or clear. Don't assume everybody instinctively understands this because they don't. Nailing the desired experience, articulating it clearly and gaining consensus or alignment is the critical first step to drive creative and channel development.

Target Tactically. The attitudes and behavior of your target population dictates everything. Understanding the psycho-demographics, experiences, practical behaviors and motivations of your target customers requires data and insight. Very few target populations are homogenous or behave consistently, so you'll have to tease out the segments and address them directly or independently.

Focus on the Big Idea. Once you know whom you're talking to and what you want them to feel and do, the search for a big creative idea kicks into high gear. What message can credibly penetrate, animate, mobilize and influence your target customers? The challenge is finding a creative concept broad enough to be communicated across channels.

Pick a Message Strategy. How will you present the message? Will it be blasted out as a roadblock across channels, kicked off with or tied to a live or streaming event, or subtly parsed among channels with variations aimed at target segments? Understanding segments and consumer behavior across channels will guide you to the optimal approach for communicating your message. Your position in the marketplace, budgets, brand awareness and the competitive arena will influence these choices.

Forecast. Brands can get a pretty fair read on their customers' interests, influences and habits. Use these in projecting how the big idea and the message strategy might be received. There is a reasonable amount of predictability in each business category. Don't ignore this data; use it. In fact, research techniques are emerging not only to test the big idea and its creative executions, but also to test which channels might be most powerful for the job.

Maximize Media Mix. Effective channel strategies begin with a clear understanding of how your target uses media compared to hypotheses about which channel best accomplishes which marketing task. It helps to understand and plan for media synergies by recognizing which channels go together, complement each other or fill in for weaknesses.

What are baseline or table stakes channels? Which have resonated well in the past? Which channels are worthy of testing? What will be your awareness vehicles? What will cater to or reward loyalists? How will you generate and nurture new leads? How can you generate buzz, mobilize influences and drive traffic or user generated content? And what is the relative weight of these tasks when measured against the business objectives of your campaign? The last question should drive budget allocations.

Optimize. Measurement is a given. Real-time measurement can lead to optimization—the agile process of responding to your audiences by maximizing the impact of media dollars spent by shifting allocations on the fly or by responding to your customers' signals. Digital media enable optimization on short notice.

Multichannel marketing is a way of strategically thinking about going-to-market rather than a cookie cutter template for messages, media, timing or budgeting. Thinking through these eight steps will increase the likelihood of success.

New Ways to Get Consumers' Attention

Getting attention is the prime directive for marketers. But digital behaviors and changing neural pathways and synapses are changing the way consumers pay attention, according to a pair of studies conducted for Microsoft.

The brain is a flexible and adaptable organ that learns and responds to new stimuli. The use of digital, social and mobile media can change the physical structure of neural processing, which ultimately impacts cognitive skills. As we change what we do and how we do it, the brain adapts. The net result is that in an always-on, multi-screen world, we pay attention differently than we used to.

The average human attention span, according to Statistic Brain, has fallen 33 percent from 12 seconds in 2000 to eight seconds in 2013—a second less than the attention span of a goldfish!

The hypothesis is that "the brain's cognitive functioning shifts in response to regular intensive use of technology." Our evolving digital lifestyles are changing our day-to-day ability to pay attention, effectively rewiring our brains. Increased digital media consumption has reduced consumers' ability to focus for extended periods of time. Simultaneously, tech savvy consumers are increasingly improving their ability to process, sort and store the torrent of information coming at them constantly on multiple devices. Our brains are adapting to new communication patterns.

The studies start with a classic academic methodology for assessing attention, the Sohlberg & Mateer model, which posits three attention styles. *Sustained Attention* maintains focus during repetitive activity. *Selective Attention* maintains attention in the face of distracting stimuli. And *Alternating Attention* shifts cognition between tasks demanding different skills. Everyone uses each style. But most people have a basic dominant attention posture.

Two thousand people in the UK and another two thousand people in Canada were measured against these attention states and surveyed about digital lifestyles.

Here's what they found.

Three Things Affect Attention. Volume, intensity and style of everyday media consumption determine attention patterns. Style is a key factor. Watching TV while tweeting, surfing or texting changes the attention profile significantly.

Tech Savvy Matters. Knowledge, confidence and experience with technology can determine whether a person pays Selective or Alternating attention. Tech familiarity drives alternating patterns.

New Attention Modes. *Attention Ninjas* compartmentalize tasks to control their environment. Specific tasks are assigned to specific devices. It's a divide and conquer attention coping strategy. *Attention Pragmatists* have a lesser degree of compartmentalization and combine tasks and devices without rigid rules. Things are sorted by device more fluidly. *Attention Ambidextrous* people routinely blend tasks and devices together. It's a universal tool strategy that combines work, home and play across devices to get economy of motion and increased productivity.

Address New Attention Modes. Ninjas have to be addressed clearly and induced to stop what they are doing and pay attention. The offer and call to action need to be clear and compelling to divert them from their immediate task.

Pragmatists have to be entertained and engaged preferably by prompting interaction to ensure they pay attention and buy in. They need to be engaged before they can focus on the message.

The ambidextrous need short, telegraphic messages that can be accessed on or responded to on multiple devices. They are natural jugglers and messages have to jump into their queue. Brands have to catch them midstream and direct them with clear and simple messages in a variety of contexts.

Shifting patterns of attention require different ways to target and address attention-oriented segments, which probably correlate to age, education, occupation and tech usage. Consumers grasp, sort and act in seconds. Getting enough consumer attention to move products or markets is increasingly difficult. Marketers must frame interactions to be clear, relevant and personal using ideas, timing and functionalities to make response and interaction easy, frictionless and fun across devices.

Everyone Needs an eCommerce Strategy

For the first time ever in 2016, online shopping surpassed in-store purchases according to a survey of 5000 shoppers conducted by UPS and Comscore.

Shoppers surveyed made 51percent of their purchases online. Forty-four percent of smartphone users purchase using their device. As you might imagine, millennial purchasing using smartphones outranked other age cohorts. Overall, 190 million Americans will shop online this year, according to the US Commerce Department, representing 11 percent of all retail spending.

Amazon will grab about 60 percent of total American online sales, while 74percent of small business don't even have an eCommerce website, according to SurePayroll's Small Business Scorecard. Walker Sand's 2016 Future of Retail Study discovered a third of online shoppers are visiting eCommerce sites weekly, driven by free shipping offers. This trend to shop and buy online will only get bigger and more nuanced as competition for a share gets more intense. Facebook's retail strategy is expected to alter the eCommerce equation.

The implication is that every business needs an eCommerce strategy and a way to satisfy the growing appetite for online shopping. Five imperatives should drive thinking about marketing strategy and technology infrastructure.

Be Available. Your brand has to be available across channels 24/7. As Sam Walton used to say, "You've got to be there whenever your customer is ready to buy." SEO and SEM are table stakes, as are compelling video content in social and mobile channels for driving inbound traffic. A robust email or CRM marketing effort gives brands the mechanism and the agility to stimulate traffic or to respond to marketplace developments.

Be Easy & Intuitive. Amazon trained a generation to expect easy-to-use navigation, product access in two clicks, detailed product information, consumer and professional reviews and 1-click purchasing. Consumers expect upsell and cross-sell offers, the chance to rate and review their purchases and the ability to see and buy from their purchase history. Most of all, consumers expect to get in, get what they want and get out quickly. This is the gold standard to meet or beat.

Be Channel Agnostic. Starbucks has built consumer muscle memory around integrated multi-channel functionality. Activity on the website, swipe cards and their apps are integrated and synchronized. Customers can use any channel interchangeably and can always see current cash and points balances. Starbucks uses all three functional channels, plus email and a points scheme, to stimulate buying and to push through product and time-sensitive promotions.

Be Relevant. Grocery chains using load-to-card technology proactively aggregate coupons, apply discounts and leverage purchase history to engage customers. The leaders have trained consumers to demand personal and relevant offers.

Consumers expect favorite brands to know them and to use what they know to selectively present offers, deals and early information or access to relevant products. Personalization is more about understanding what people like and what people want or want to buy rather than addressing them by name.

Be Rewarding. Shopping has a practical and a psychological aspect. The experience is everything. Craft a frictionless brand shopping experience so that customers feel good about what they bought and how they bought it. Most eCommerce experiences end in either satisfaction or frustration; the latter doom brands to immediate irrelevance.

Understand customers' mindset, behaviors and shopping journey. Many brands dole out reward points or discounts based on purchase volumes or thresholds. Yet in spite of the proliferation of point schemes, the jury is out on the real margin or ROI value of these tactics in promoting repeat business, grabbing added market share or activating brand loyalty.

Demand stimulation, research, shopping and ongoing customer relationships are happening online across channels with social and mobile playing an increasing role. Patterns of use are varied, individual and idiosyncratic. This requires brands to re-think go-to-market and eCommerce strategies and makes strategic technology investments necessary to keep up with customers and fend off the Amazon colossus.

Future Proof Your Brand

Brands seeking to future-proof their marketing have to anticipate rapid and radical changes to the marketing landscape and the technology arena. The only constant is consumers' need for genuine, reliable and relatable brands.

Authenticity. Brands have to be what they say they are. Dealings with consumers must be clear, transparent, straightforward and friendly. Brands have to be willing and able to interact with customers, listen, respond and engage. A customer-first mentality is a must at every level.

People Panel. Brands cannot afford to lose touch with their best customers and prospects. The future will belong to brands that can regularly understand their customers' journey, find the appropriate language and inflection points, nimbly adjust to changing mores, and consistently deliver relevance, utility and value.

Whether it's a standing panel, ad hoc panels, focus groups, clubs, CRM/loyalty programs, mall intercepts, eye-tracking, MRI/brain waves, ethnographic studies, live spy-cams or even telepathic communication, brands need to be in touch and up to the moment with customers' needs, wants, likes, dislikes, fears and hopes. Brands that don't institutionalize ways to tap these sentiments and keep abreast of the changing culture, globally and market-by-market, will be left behind.

Omnichannel Agility. Sam Walton was right! You have to engage consumers whenever and wherever they want. This means covering the obvious bases and routinely testing and experimenting with whatever shiny new object catches the fancy of your best customers. Today, it's social and mobile. Tomorrow, it will be wearables or implants, or more sophisticated variations on the channels we know.

Seasoned Teams. The best way to future-proof a brand is to create a stable of trusted advisors and resources who can learn, grow and improve over time. This is an anathema in today's environment. Brands need to build and maintain best-in-class marketing ecosystems, comprising teams that work together and know each other over time. Teams that collectively understand consumers, markets and channels and are able to creatively deploy the talents of specialists in any situation.

Brands must marry agencies or consultants or technologists to create sustainable, adaptable relationships that can anticipate and react to a wide range of possibilities. Talent, commitment to common goals, muscle memory and institutional insight are critical assets in short supply. But they are building blocks for the future.

Secure Atomized and Automatic Data. The future requires using data strategically, in real time, to create millions of one-to-one messages and marketing plans. The gating factor is collecting and processing data efficiently and effectively, which means investments in three critical technologies.

Security and encryption are table stakes for keeping and using personal information. Atomization, or the ability to keep data sets in a neutral state where they can be easily transferred and ingested into new software, will alter our reliance on legacy systems and give us flexibility to use the latest, fastest or smartest new platforms.

Artificial Intelligence plus Automation, now in its infancy, will be second nature in the future. Consumers will expect brands to know them and know them well, by instantly accessing directive or predictive data to find the right moment and send the right message to the right person in their preferred channel. Tweaking algorithms and building fuzzy logic to trigger messaging based on behavior is the Holy Grail that will be consistently sought and probably found, most likely brand-by-brand.

Nobody can predict the future with any certainty. But brands can prepare themselves to face relentless change and regular innovation by focusing on these five future-proofing fundamentals.

Maximizing Media Mix

Marketers are constantly tweaking and optimizing tactical plans, purchase orders and cash flow models in the quest for the ultimate media mix. This necessitates constant monitoring of channels to enable nimble choices focused on audience dynamics or response, channel innovations, media synergies and targeting strategy. Creating the right mix is a puzzle unique to each brand.

Approaching the task, several truths need to be considered:

- Each channel has strengths, weaknesses and optimal uses
- Business objectives must drive the process
- Clarity is critical. You have to know what you want to happen at the outset
- Matching target customers and prospects with media use yields efficiency
- Social and mobile media are ascendant and inter-related
- Assume significant mobile use
- Search and E-mail are undervalued, but proven performers
- Recognize the difference between engagement and conversion

A new way of conceptualizing the marketing mix is emerging that looks at three lines of attack, orchestrated to operate independently and inter-dependently. Online and offline marketing are planned together and synchronized to ensure that the brand speaks with a single voice to achieve maximum reach, frequency and impact. The application of machine learning will constantly update the data and drive continuous learning and optimization.

Owned media are brand assets and tightly controlled real estate represented by brand websites, your blog or YouTube channel, Facebook or Twitter pages, unique games or functionality deployed across the web, a consumer database and its attendant opt-in permissions. These assets become the canvas for presenting the brand story in all its nuanced detail and for creating or using content to systematically and continuously engage customers and prospects.

Paid Media are a variety of display, social and mobile ad units in a mix of contextual landscapes purchased from third parties, that give brands the opportunity to integrate themselves into customer lifestyles and/or work flow patterns. Paid media can be integrated or interruptive and can use a wide array of tactics, including content creation, to drive traffic to owned assets or engage and enroll customers directly.

Earned Media is the result of consumer engagement and resonance; those added impressions and viral pass-alongs that happen when a brand genuinely connects with its customer base. This can be partially planned but is often serendipitous. Earned media is the report card for how well a brand orchestrates its owned and paid media.

Some of the growing channels are not instantly available or fully mature. Mobile access is growing exponentially, as is the desire for deals, yet not all audiences are eager to check-in or download coupons. Demographics dictate mobile readiness. The older your audience, the less likely they are ready for mobile campaigns.

In the race to grasp new advertising opportunities, the likely reach, frequency and effectiveness must be evaluated in terms of the overlap between channel users and a brand's most likely customers and prospects. Then the trade-off from what worked in the past to what might work in the future must be forecast. In this context, Facebook, with its enormous reach and selective targeting capabilities, looks like a safe bet in spite of the company's aspirations for ultimate control of advertising and their unwillingness to share data.

As you structure your marketing, consider four vectors when evaluating the effectiveness of your choices.

Business Effectiveness. Nothing counts if you don't sell what you need to sell. Marketing expenditures need to be measured against business goals by plotting the return on investment, calculating the margins and assessing the cost of sale in comparison to the anticipated profit.

Communications Impact. Is your message getting through? These are the classic brand measures of message relevance and persuasion, A&U, brand awareness, preference and intention to buy.

Media Efficiency. Are you getting the most bang for each buck? Measure the effective reach by counting the cost-per-thousand, the click-thru rates. Then calculate the impact by looking at the cost-per-acquisition/retention/sale and by comparing this data with cost-per-click.

Brand Equity. Are you winning hearts and minds? The Net Promoter Score is becoming the benchmark although many marketers also assess customer satisfaction and calculate brand loyalty based on repeat purchases, referrals or redeemed offers.

Nobody has nailed the most effective media mix...yet. But understanding the landscape and rigorously measuring the value of investments will give you pretty good insight into the effectiveness and efficiency of your campaigns.

Mobilizing Influencers

Who has more consumer influence: your Uncle Bob, a favorite blogger or Kim Kardashian?

This is the word-of-mouth marketing question marketers keep asking. The desire to gain access and influence by borrowing relationships and equity has become a cottage industry, loosely called "influencer marketing." Originally the province of PR guys, everyone is now into the influencer act, even though it's not particularly clear how to define influence, who really has it, how we measure it and when or how it should be deployed it for optimum payoff.

The desire to efficiently expand reach and frequency in social networks has led marketers to search for ways to leverage "influence." Ideally, if we can identify the best influencers, brands can co-opt them or rent them and use their networks to spread the word with increased speed and credibility at modest costs. This has been a fantasy since the first blog appeared.

The problem is there are too many unknowns:

- There is no standard definition of influence.
- Influence is a by-product of a trusted relationship.
- Influence can be fleeting, categorical or contingent.
- Influence happens in context and in the moment.
- Influence waxes and wanes over time.
- Influence works both ways and is often weighted by degrees.
- Other factors (e.g. urgency) magnify or diminish the impact of influence.
- Few people hold sway over others for sustained periods of time.
- Influence is mitigated by experience.
- Influencers can give bad advice or direction.
- Influence can impact awareness and preference but fall short of sales.
- Overexposure (Kim Kardashian or Neil Patrick Harris) diminishes influence.

- Influencers can be shills or undisclosed paid pitchmen, not neutral observers.

Entering into the fray is Dr. Jonah Berger of the Wharton School at University of Pennsylvania, sponsored by Experticity.com and the Keller Fay Group. These guys surveyed 6000 people from their expert list and the general public to get a read on influence and influencers. They wanted to know if celebrities or others have the most useful influence.

Their findings—that Uncle Bob, now labeled a "micro influencer," wins—is a tad self-serving, yet nonetheless interesting and possibly true.

Micro influencers, defined as "a person who has a greater than average reach or impact through word of mouth in a relevant marketplace," have 22 times more conversations about purchasing recommendations than the average person. And 82 percent of consumers polled said they were highly likely to follow these recommendations.

This makes common sense. People who are seriously into something (photography, genealogy, music, etc.) talk about it incessantly, study everything they can find on the topic and attract people who want more information from an un-branded neutral source. These self-proclaimed experts are rarely bashful. Almost everybody has a go-to guy on different subjects who can be relied upon to know the latest and greatest and have a point of view. So, it's not surprising that 87 percent of the influencer recommendations in this study were delivered face-to-face and that these influencers were considered more credible than the average person.

Influence is an elusive concept and an elusive measurement. This survey casts doubt on the value of celebrity or social media star posts and tweets versus lesser-known bloggers and Uncle Bob. It's a step in the right direction because getting a better handle on influence, those who wield it and how it impacts subsequent downrange buying behavior, is high on our marketing agenda.

B2B Marketers–Pick Up the Phone!

Obsessed by digital, social and mobile media, B2B marketers chronically underestimate the value of the telephone. Outbound telemarketers are critical for any B2B business.

The first decision is to buy or rent. In most cases, skilled outsiders understand not only know how to use the phone effectively but how large organizations work and how to get inside them for maximum effect. In my experience, contract teams outperform traditional inside sales guys because they have veteran players, are better managed, organized, disciplined and trained as hunters.

Highly motivated, because they are rewarded on performance, outsourced telemarketers commit to service level agreements (SLAs). They deliver a fixed scope of work at an agreed price. And they have sophisticated tools to measure, monitor and optimize campaigns in real time.

Many of my clients have no benchmarks to measure outside calling specialists against inside guys. They usually can't tell me how many dials, calls and successful outcomes the inside guys do each day, week or month. They rarely can redirect their teams against a new or different target quickly and, too often, there are turf wars and politics that cloud the relationship between inside sales and field sales or marketing teams.

Consider two cases to illustrate the value and utility of a seasoned outbound calling team.

Fast Market Insight. One client is crafting a new positioning and value proposition aimed at a specific, narrow swath of the market. Before we commit significant time, effort and cash to the new concepts or a new campaign, we want to test the new concepts against likely buyers, Vice Presidents and Directors at Fortune 1000 companies to see if our big ideas resonate.

We compiled a list of 1000 companies and target titles based on a "best prospect" profile. We purchased lists against those names, fully expecting 30-45percent of the names to be wrong, and wrote a six-question survey to test our messages. Our outside calling team promised to get 100 completed interviews in 20 business days.

Fast-forward 20 days. 100 interviews are complete; the data is collected, analyzed and displayed in snappy charts and graphs. We got our answers and are actively revising our go-to-market story, based on the feedback. Every respondent fit the profile, every respondent worked for a firm that is fully capable of being a real prospect. We now have the benefit of what our market is thinking and real-time intelligence about specific prospect firms, without telegraphing our moves. Add to that updated lists and contact information plus a survey performance benchmark.

Generate Leads Quickly. A second client has a product that works particularly well in manufacturing companies. This product isn't their main offering or their best seller and doesn't command the resources that it's more productive cousins enjoy.

Enter the five-member calling team. After briefing them on the product, the target market and the competitive set, we compiled a list of target companies and titles and asked them to get us 50 one-hour sales appointments in 30 days. We carefully defined criteria for qualification, which was reinforced in the call guides. With access to our Salesforce.com application they could do all the scheduling and all the data updating work as they made the calls.

At the end of 30 days we booked 56 appointments with exactly the kind of companies we asked for. We had updated and accurate records for 1000 target companies as well as a lot of useful information about how people reacted to our brand, our product and our competitors. The performance of the outside team, which had 10 hours of orientation and training on the product and the brand, was 5 times better than our inside sales guys, all of whom have been with the firm more than two years.

A telephone in the right hands is a business development power tool. Used properly, it gives you reach, insight and access at predictable speeds. There is nothing in the B2B marketing arsenal as powerful.

Don't Write Off Direct Mail

Direct mail volume is down. Big traditional mailers are scaling back. Costs are up. Postal rates keep rising. But targeted and personalized direct mail can be a breakthrough medium.

Here's why...

1. We're inundated with e-mail. There's little magic, no anticipation and few new tricks to surprise us and to prompt more, better opens. We're even immune to flashing emojis. E-mail has become institutionalized and response rates have plateaued.
2. Nobody gets personal mail. Of the 200 billion pieces of mail that the post office delivers, less than 3 percent is actual personal, relevant human-to- human content. Mail is an underused channel. The clear implication (at least to me) is that if you write somebody a personal letter -- one that looks, feels and smells like a personal letter (not an ad in an envelope) using personal, individualized information in the body copy-- you have a shot at genuinely touching and communicating with a customer or prospect. It's a rare chance to capitalize on the unexpected.
3. Tested creative tactics exist. Direct mailers have tested and refined an array of techniques to optimize opens and response -- the twin moments of truth. We have a corpus of knowledge on the size, shape, texture, color, fonts, forms of address, key words and tone of voice to use to address discrete audiences. The trick is to blend this expertise with purchase history or behavioral data to create a compelling, relevant, personal, maybe even intimate form of communication. This is a primary application of Big Data. The technology to do this, and still make it look private, individual and personal, is widely available.
4. Small batch targeting. While the big volume mailers and carpet bombers are cutting back and scrambling to survive, returning to the basic letter format gives marketers a perfect

platform for targeting and testing. Even with a medium that costs 10 times more than e-mail, even small firms can afford to word process and mail hundreds or thousands of carefully selected and targeted names. Whether the focus is acquisition, retention, loyalty or usage stimulation, a personal letter can cost effectively move the needle.

5. The first mover wins. Because so many direct marketers are bombing customers and prospects with self-mailers, double-sided postcards, snap-packs, letter packages that scream "I'm an ad" on the envelope, coupons, flyers, catalogs, circulars, postcards, faux invitations, faux greeting cards, faux bills, faux official documents and all kinds of other printed SPAM, the victory will go to the first mover who does it right because it will be so different and unexpected.
6. Leverage remembered joy. As children we were all surprised and delighted by something that came to us in the mail from someone special far away. The memory and the feelings of that moment are stored and carried around by millions of people. A well-crafted personal letter taps the reservoir of good will and belief that these memories represent. Mail, more than pixels, carry embedded emotions. These impulses and sentiments can be directed your way.

SECTION II

CRM / ENGAGEMENT / LOYALTY

Loyalty is a Function of Love & Money

In an over-saturated, over-messaged, fast moving highly competitive omnichannel marketplace, building a loyal customer base of people who buy regularly and advocate for their favorite brands is an imperative. Acquiring, retaining, mobilizing, motivating and incenting loyalty over time is a question of love and money.

Brands have had an off-and-on relationship with CRM and loyalty marketing over the years. Every brand attracts loyalists. It costs 5-10 times more to find a new customer than it does to resell an existing customer. Most brands fantasize about identifying, motivating and rewarding the 20 percent of customers who generate 80 percent of the sales.

Loyalists buy more, buy more often and tell everyone they know about the brands they love. Building and sustaining loyalty is part stimulus-and-response, part value exchange and part emotional experience. The quality of the relationship rather than the number or value of transactions is the barometer for loyalty.

Love and money are the two drivers, the levers and currencies that power loyalty marketing. The concepts are simple. The execution is technically and psychologically complex.

Most people have a finite reservoir of affinities. Nobody loves everybody and everything. There are brands we care deeply about, brands we generally or occasionally prefer, and lots of brands we don't know or don't really care about until a moment of truth presents itself and we are forced to make a choice. The drivers of brand attachments and connections range from childhood or sensory experiences to convenience and utility to badge or status value.

Consumers like what they like on their own terms. Enthusiasms wax and wane. They want to hear from brands – but not that often. They are governed by a WiiFM (what's in it for me) mentality, even for brands near and dear to their hearts. Long-standing loyalty can be derailed by aggressive price offers or a bad product, retail or customer service interaction.

The trick to designing an effective loyalty program is to apportion love and money for maximum business impact. People who love your brand need to feel connected and appreciated. They need to know that their connection is acknowledged, valued and reciprocal. They don't need an incentive; they're going to buy anyway. They need a sign of love to reinforce and mobilize their loyalty. They need to be cued and to be coddled.

They crave inside or exclusive information, early access to new products or services, private trunk shows, personal shoppers, private 800 numbers and mini-sites, first dibs on your best offerings and opportunities, to beta test products or give input into offerings in your pipeline. They want to be a part of what your brand is doing.

And they expect you to know who they are, their favorite location, their sizes, their style preferences and even their means of payment. Loyalists expect favorite brands to know and act on what they've previously bought and what they might be interested in next. Hyper sensitive to the tone of your communications, they are open to suggestions and recommendations and judge your moves by the degree of relevance, convenience and personalization they reflect.

Consumers who split their loyalty or are ambivalent about your brand need money to motivate them. Some will become loyalists. Most can be convinced to make additional incremental one-time purchases with a relevant, valuable offer at the right time and in the right tone of voice. This becomes a test-and-learn exercise to find the right offer value that yields optimum revenue.

Knowing whom to mobilize to achieve incremental spending is the KPI. Apply coupons, special deals, BOGOs, rebates and price incentives where it will do the most good soonest. Recency and frequency of interaction will yield clues to finding the best segment to incent with money offers. Most often those most likely to act on your offer are aware and slightly engaged with your brand but split their affinity based on any number of factors.

In most cases, high propensity buyers will look a lot like a lighter version of your loyalists on a psycho-demographic basis. The smart guys build propensity and mirror models to optimize performance and zero in on those most likely to yield new or incremental revenues. Money is used as a lever to change or direct behavior.

In a plugged-in, on-the-go, ADD society where everyone is a connected critic, loyalty is a constantly shifting bogey. Yet brands can capitalize on the longing for connection, recognition and reward by thoughtfully and scientifically allocating love and money.

Addressing On-Demand Consumers

Technology breakthroughs plus ADD and constant information overload has transformed us into an on-demand society. Americans expect instant, everywhere, anytime access and immediate gratification. This is a cultural sea change for marketers, most of whom share the consumer psychology but haven't yet applied it to their businesses.

We expect to be able to get, do or be almost anything, whenever the idea strikes us. Limitless goods or services should be available or come automatically to us, reflecting our interests, needs, preferences, purchase histories and personalities. The remarkable thing is, as documented in MDC Partners' report entitled "Popular By Demand", that doctors, limos and taxis, movies, food delivery, house cleaners, dog walkers and an array of other services actually deliver on this desire. The aggregation and synchronization of digital functionalities combined with real-time Big Data processing will make these conveniences and utilities increasingly more available, efficient and embedded in our everyday lives.

On-demand requires that the consumer control everything. We select the products or services we want. We reject any bundle or package that we haven't personally constructed. We pay only for what we want, what we use or when we want or use it. We crave every deal, every efficiency and every angle. Each choice is spontaneous or impromptu. We reject long-term connections, memberships, subscriptions, affiliations or commitments unless there is a compelling incentive. Brand loyalty is earned, lost and measured in nanoseconds.

This a la carte mentality comes with a side order of limited patience. Things must be fast, accurate, friendly, correct, working properly, flexible and to our liking. We won't wait long for anything. And we can broadcast satisfaction and praise or dissatisfaction and detailed complaints in two clicks anytime and anywhere.

We are demanding, impatient consumers short on time, overwhelmed with stimuli and desperate for anything that can be seamlessly incorporated into our social and mobile lifestyle to help us. We expect to use mobile devices as universal tools to manage our busy lives. Many on-demand concierge services are being delivered by mobile apps and many more are planned as Geoffrey A. Fowler pointed out in The Wall Street Journal. To respond and leverage this on-demand psychology, consider three key tactics.

Build a Smorgasbord. Think about how your brand can display its assets day in and day out, across channels or devices, for maximum on-demand access, transparency and utility. Tier offerings so consumers can assess value, choose to pay premium prices for premium services and build their own packages. On-demand users are willing to pay an average of 14percent more over traditional services. Dynamic pricing can also focus on peak times, limited offerings, unique styles, heightened services or perishability.

Imagine your customers eagerly working their way around a brimming smorgasbord table and emerging with bulging plates. Put the sweet or savory lures, with high margin potential, front and center. Then monitor and measure uptake.

When I worked with Dell in the 1990s, the brand differentiator and value proposition was to build your own computer. But after analyzing thousands of transactions, we discovered that 70 percent of consumers built the same computer. Use on-demand behavior to anticipate and mirror consumer needs, reduce buying friction, re-position brands and expedite customer delight.

Address Chronic Shortages. Nobody has enough time, money, energy, insight, convenience or patience. Convenience, luxury and need are three prominent on-demand drivers. Position and structure your brand offerings to answer these unmet needs. Create comparisons. Do the math for your prospects. Merchandise features and benefits in terms of alleviating consumer pain points. Be faster, easier, more available, more intuitive or more valuable. Be explicit in explaining how your brand delivers the extras that consumers crave.

Connect the Dots. Link your on-demand offering with others to mirror how people think, act and shop. Uber has linked with TripAdvisor, United Airlines, Hyatt Hotels and Open Table to create a service-oriented ecosystem that anticipates and cross-promotes the full range of travel needs. Use APIs and social log-ins to connect data sets and enable 1-click access.

GPS Shopper CEO Alex Muller emphasizes the importance of proximity, personalization and responsiveness to increase revenue and enhance the customer experience. Put yourself in your customers' shoes. Figure out what products and services logically and practically fit together. Then build a brand-centered network to deliver them.

On-demand is the new normal. It's not going away. In fact, the pressure to deliver more and more things on-demand will grow exponentially as bandwidth and technology becomes faster, more universal and sophisticated. Brands that don't recognize this fundamental attitudinal shift and address it directly will be left in the dust.

Improving Engagement Planning

Engagement is a term that means everything and nothing. It's used offensively, defensively or indiscriminately to thrust or parry arguments about strategy, technology, media or creative.

Engagement is the desired human interaction that results from marketing activity. It is a feeling, a thought or an action that a person takes in response to a branded experience—messaging or functionality.

Engagement planning starts with the desired response in mind and then maps customer attitudes and behaviors to find relevant and appropriate inflection points to begin the conversation. Engagement planning doesn't start with tactics or channels. It starts with an understanding of what real people are likely to feel, think or do in response to a stimulus.

To enter the conversation and frame an initial message, marketers need to consider these five factors.

Creature Cycles. We are creatures of habit. We do things in predictable ways. Standard behavior patterns include where we go, how we get there, what we expect, what we do and in what sequence we undertake tasks. Most of us prioritize tasks and people in repeatable ways.

Understanding internal drivers and external influences affecting target audiences allow us to find openings for marketing. The goal is to find ways to intersect the lives and life patterns of customers and prospects that synch up with what they do, want, need or expect. The first step in planning engagement is to figure out how to be relevant and useful.

Standing. Openness to people and ideas is a function of familiarity and standing. If I know and respect you, I'm much more open to you than if you are a complete stranger. Brands are sorted into discrete folders in our brains. You have to know how you are sorted and what standing you have to enter into the conversation. An athletic wear brand can probably speak credibly about exercise and wellness, less so about politics or cultural issues.

Brands have less standing than friends, coworkers or family members. The level of credibility, awareness, interest and trust in a brand, basically how brands are sorted, determines the aperture you have for reaching target customers.

Engagement planning has to begin with an assessment of your standing which might lead to the decision to borrow standing from those with better connections or connotations—influencers or current members. High awareness brands have more standing than invisibles or newbies.

Standing defines the angle of attack. A complete stranger approaching customers using personal information or outsized claims prompts immediate revulsion and rejection. Getting good juicy gossip from a trusted friend is the opposite end of the spectrum. Plotting your standing will separate intrusive from invited messages.

Posture. There are many ways to approach customers. Usually the approach is a function of the state of the relationship. In some cases a message delivered by a credible third party has more impact than a direct approach. In the case of brand loyalists, whispering insider or advanced information in their ears builds demand, satisfaction and loyalty faster. And for those actively shopping, eye-to-eye, direct offers can drive faster conversion. Posture affects the psychology of your positioning and shapes the tone, manner, language and attitude of creative.

Timing. Timing is everything. Texting a busy mom at 7 am while she's trying to get her kids up, dressed, fed and out the door is a non-starter. Brands need to understand the mindset and the mechanics of customers' lives. As mobile becomes the ubiquitous on-the-go channel of choice, timing, utility and relevance become critical success factors. Marketers must get much more intimate with the routes and routines of target audiences.

UXD. Any desired action must be fast, easy to do, intuitive and simple to understand. Account for distractions, fat fingers and multi-tasking. Messages must drive to simple desired actions. Labels on buttons and CTAs must be clear and telegraphic.

Buttons have to be big and colored. Copy has to be scan-able and snack-able. Increase the font size. Don't skimp on white space. Pressure test every sequence. Invest heavily in connecting all the data pipes on the back end. If you get everything else right but blow the user experience design, you lose the ballgame.

Engagement is about genuine human connection. Channels, media, content and technology are facilitators. The ultimate measurement is a thought, a feeling or an action.

Customer Experience According to Chef Bouley

David Bouley is arguably one of the greatest American chefs. He is also a god when it comes to designing a customer experience. Dining at his eponymous restaurant in the Tribeca neighborhood of Manhattan was a sensation for the pallet and a practical lesson in how to consciously design an experience to surprise and delight.

Customer intimacy and experience are the buzzwords and aspirations of the moment. The increasing availability of analytics and data to support and direct creative and design choices point to more personal, relevant, useful and delightful ways for brands to engage, sell and build advocacy among consumers.

Here's what I learned from a master chef:

Target the Business Objective. Everything begins with what you want the customer to see, feel and take away. Bouley wants you to walk away feeling amazing. He will fill your mouth with tastes and sensations you've never had before. He'll surround you with warmth, comfort and a sense of understated luxury that leaves you with the feeling that you are welcomed and belong. He focuses on you and your guests by providing a platform to share and converse. And he sends you into the night happy and satisfied with free, unexpected and delicious provisions for breakfast. Bouley built a loyal customer base for his expense account restaurant by starting with the business objective in mind.

Focus on Senses and Cadences. Most experiences have a beginning, a middle and an end. Bouley guides what you see, hear, smell, feel and taste. Bouley instinctively understands the importance of emotion and feeling in the marketing process. Nothing is left to chance. The entry way smells of warm apples. The room is warm and lit sensuously. The chairs are extremely comfortable. The linens are crisp but not overly starched. The menu reflects seasonal tastes and locally available fresh seasonal ingredients.

The experience is designed to be frictionless. Everything is gently revealed and pleasant. The stumbling blocks have been anticipated and proactively cleared. The people who greet you are formal but friendly. Every element is orchestrated to give you a feeling of belonging and to heighten your enjoyment in the moment.

The food comes out at a pace that feels natural. You never wait too little or too long. The staff watches closely to see when you pause, when you're done or when you need more water, bread or wine. He super delivers against expectations. You expect a waiter; you get a team. You expect bread; you get a bread cart with twenty choices and a doting baker. You expect a drink, an appetizer, an entree and a dessert; you get that plus an array of unexpected tastes and mini-courses punctuated by explanations by the maître d.

Get the Details Right. Consumers are influenced by initial impressions, comfortable design and intuitive navigation. The only way to deliver these experiences is to develop a laser-like focus on the details. Bouley thinks about ambient light, the feel of the napkins, the weight of the fish forks, the shape of the water and wine glasses and the mother-of-pearl check carrier.

If you are serious about optimizing the customer experience and fostering engagement and satisfaction, translate the Bouley strategy into digital channels by doing these seventeen things:

- Decide what you want prospects to see, think and feel
- Focus on what your customers want and where they look
- Anticipate what they expect to do
- Track what they actually do
- Imagine all the things that could get in the way
- Look how they search and what words they use
- Watch how they scroll, click or download
- Measure which elements get the most engagement or time spent
- Think long and hard about where you place the CTAs; their size, color, and labels
- Test fonts, type sizes and kerning
- Assess page views and page sequences
- Get feedback as you design experiences
- Group like content or products for easy comparison or upsell
- Install pixel tracking or metrics software
- Test your designs with eye-tracking and guided tasks

- Keep your eye on what competitors are doing
- Look out the window. Learn from unusual experts like David Bouley.

5 Deadly Lead Generation Sins

Making and receiving cold calls is a nightmare. Engaging strangers is the toughest part of B2B lead generation. But there are ways to get access and ways to be instantly disqualified. Unfortunately, large numbers of would-be partners or vendors use email and LinkedIn to annoy rather than to enchant prospective customers.

There are countless numbers of firms scattered across the globe offering IT services, web development, media buying, creative services, lists, lead generation, design, video, audio, graphics and broadcast production, fulfillment or administrative services. Competition is fierce. And genuine need is random and unpredictable. Therefore, cold calling is a necessity.

Here are 5 deadly lead generation sins to avoid.

Don't Pretend You Know Me. It starts with a connection or a friend request. An affirmative response triggers an instant, but ignorant pitch. The language is friendly, chatty and off-putting. Some salespeople assume that common group membership creates a family relationship. It doesn't. We both joined a group. We're not cousins.

Don't Do Any Homework. I get 10 - 20 emails a week from firms that are either competitive with mine or completely out of our ecosystem. Sprinkling a company name into a generic pitch never impresses anyone. Look at our website. Try to get a feel for what we do and which clients we serve. Then figure out if your product or service is logically connected. Never assume we need what you're peddling.

Don't Read Into Titles. I have had grand titles. It suggests a much greater decision-making role than I actually have. Beware of terms like director, digital, strategy or ranks above VP. They mean very different things in different organizations. Don't assume that a person who is an EVP of Digital has marketing, advertising, HR, recruiting, administrative, IT, logistics and research responsibilities. More than half of the solicitations I get are for things I have no interest in or no responsibility for.

Don't Schedule a Meeting. Presumptive meeting invitations or offers of meetings or promises of 15-minute phone calls are a huge turn off. Prospects are busy. And you are intruding. Proactively attempting to hijack my time earns an instant deletion. Persistent follow-up earns a nasty-gram.

Don't Ask Me to Tell You About My Company. The faux diagnostic approach—I tell you my troubles and you offer up solutions—only works if I invite you to talk in the first place. Asking me to educate you about my needs is a waste of time especially if you're an unwanted, uninvited stranger. Asking me to pass you along to the right person is a no-go.

The key to getting access is to know whom you're addressing and provocatively dangle something new, different, intriguing, relevant or personal. Avoid pretense. Avoid a bland generic listing of products or services. Don't assume anything about my needs or me. Avoid these five deadly sins.

The Impact of Surprise and Delight!

There is a particular joy in being recognized and rewarded by a favorite brand. This bonding feeling is heightened when it's completely unexpected or delivered in an unusual way.

I'm a classical music fan and symphony subscriber, admittedly a dwindling population. I build my own subscription to the New York Philharmonic, usually by selecting the cheapest orchestra seats six to eight times a year. As a result, I get a slew of email, direct mail and prospecting calls from the NY Phil. Sometimes it feels like they are desperate for my next purchase and/or anxious to reel in anyone younger than 80 to attend the concerts.

Recently, on entering David Geffen Hall, my wife I and scanned our tickets and were directed aside to a table. Initially, we thought we'd been selected for extra security screening. Instead, a pleasant 20- something young woman in a simple black dress greeted us by name, thanked us profusely for being subscribers and told us how much we meant to the Philharmonic. She closed by handing us a gift.

Being a skeptical marketer, I was surprised, happy and anxious. Could the symphony be in such bad financial shape that my minor contribution made a difference? The gift was a fold up bag that my mother-in-law would love. It was a lovely unexpected gesture. I had a momentary warm and fuzzy sensation and headed to our seats.

As we got to our seats, in the back of the orchestra on the aisle, there was an envelope addressed to us taped to our seats. Our seatmates didn't have one and were eager to see what had been left for us. The envelope contained a fridge magnet, a coupon for a baseball cap and a "personal" note with a photo from Richard Deane, Associate Principal Horn. He thanked us for attending the concert, thanked us for making a contribution and assured us that "our goal onstage is to provide you with an amazing concert experience.... I hope you enjoy the performance tonight, and I look forward to seeing you at many more."

Whoa! Now we felt like VIPs, especially after the people behind, in front and to the sides seemed to be unusually curious and jealous that we had been singled out. The tactic worked without an explicit solicitation. We added two concerts to our plans when we got home! The NY Phil stoked our brand loyalty, generated word-of-mouth among our friends and added to our lifetime value at minimal cost.

The marketing lessons are:

1. Identify customers worthy of cultivating
2. Focus on those who can become best customers
3. Decide what you want them to feel, think and do
4. Surprise them when they least expect it
5. Put a human face on the interaction
6. Use multiple channels – online and offline
7. Calibrate the reward with current or lifetime value
8. Create an experience that people will share and talk about

Too many marketers get hung up on the costs and mechanics of surprising and delighting their best or high potential customers. It's about acknowledgement and engagement. It's about creating a customer experience that makes someone feel good in ways leading to brand loyalty and advocacy. The New York Philharmonic, working on a tight budget, proves this tactic can be used with minimal investment and maximum impact.

The Problem with Points

Marketers love them. They confuse consumers in spite of the fact that the average American household has 21 total and 8 or 9 active loyalty memberships. Billions of points are awarded. Most points go unredeemed. Yet, new loyalty points-based schemes are launched all the time. It's a classic disconnect.

The conventional wisdom is that points programs deliver recognition, status, intimacy and loyalty for the cost of accounting for points, reward items and frequent customer communication. Marketers believe that individuals who collect points buy more, buy more often and tell all their friends about the brand and their status. But since every hotel brand, car rental company, bank, credit card issuer and big box or chain retail merchant jumped into the points-for-loyalty game, the real and perceived value of points, rewards and even loyalty have become muddled and downgraded.

Airlines introduced points. And, later, they killed the golden goose. They set the bar high for gaining status and rewards, and then, subsequently and systematically, reduced the rewards and the status power and prestige of points. What was once a symbol of elite achievement has become a common expectation.

If you doubt me, watch as planes get boarded. More than half the line has some kind of status, which downgrades the whole point of the exercise. If points don't make you feel special and don't get you perks and benefits denied to others, what's the point? As a result of countless airline manipulations, all points programs have suffered a perceptual downfall.

Here are the principal reasons why.

Value Exchange Imbalance. One of the biggest issues is the discrepancy between earning and burning points. Many programs award points at $1 per point. Yet on redemption the values are significantly lower. My 98, 853 AMEX Gold points, earned at a dollar per point, were worth $729 or 7/100s of a cent on redemption.

According to Stacey Cowley, writing in *The New York Times*, "The general trend within loyalty and points programs is that card issuers are quick to ditch benefits that dig too deeply into their profit."

Arbitraging this difference delights marketers and frustrates consumers. Too often the value of rewards feels way out of proportion to the money spent to earn them, and the value of the rewards themselves seem irrelevant or disproportionately expensive compared to retail or discounted prices. Spending 30,000 points for a $30 coffeemaker makes many consumers crazy.

Uncertain Currency. Loyalty points are a form of virtual currency. But they only work if the value of the currency is widely understood and accepted. Many marketers launch points programs without sufficiently cueing the participating customers. Many launch programs without sounding out high value customers.

"Loyalty marketers," says Ms. Cowley, "adjust the perks of each program so often the value of miles and points changes frequently, often without warning or advance notice."

In some cases, customers are completely unaware they are enrolled in a points program, until a statement appears. I mysteriously earned 254,000 Verizon Smart Rewards. I have no idea how I racked up this total. But when I went to buy a new smartphone at the Verizon store, they were not useable. So who cares what they're worth or what they can buy!

Delayed Gratification. Like air miles, many point schemes require considerable time and purchases to accumulate enough points to earn a reward. Too often the lag time between earning and burning is not worth the wait. (The new Chase Sapphire Card was launched to directly counter this perception and to add interoperability of points as a competitive advantage.) Yet, in a world of instant communication, instant messaging and real-time eCommerce, waiting to accumulate points has limited appeal and limited incentive value.

Savvy retailers like Walgreens have converted points systems for immediate or quick in-store redemption. Target, now launching an app-based rewards program, is following suit. Amazon, arguably the biggest US retailer, has no points program.

Ease of Use. Points aren't easy to use. Finding an open eligibility window to redeem air miles requires not only superior timing and telepathic skills, but it also requires an additional ante of cash. Add that to complex redemption formulas, second-rate customer service, and it often feels that the process of redemption is purposely and rigidly constructed to frustrate customers and reduce redemption. More frequent customers are frustrated than delighted by this process.

Points programs will not disappear. So savvy marketers need to re-engineer programs by focusing on customer experience and lifestyle inflection points, eliminating bureaucratic friction, putting on a much friendlier face and building more relevant and meaningful tiers and rewards.

SECTION III

BIG DATA / MARTECH

The Basic Challenge of Big Data

The promise of Big Data—unleashing timely, relevant, useful, personal and valuable communications—is only realized if basic mechanical and processing issues are resolved.

The challenge in using Big Data is that it doesn't always fit together easily or neatly, especially when it's collected in divergent formats on different platforms. The first critical step in using Big Data is getting the data into usable forms. This is the foundational detailed technical work that makes Big Data ultimately sexy.

Here is the critical path.

Normalization. Data is collected different ways in different channels. Figuring out which data element goes with which record, assigning master IDs and getting them into a software platform that can combine structured and unstructured data is job one. This requires cleaning the data so that the fields align, the abbreviations are the same and postal, email and social addresses, plus mobile numbers, are properly formatted. It also requires constant updating since many of these data points change frequently.

Matching. Devising logistic algorithms and using fuzzy logic to build robust individual records are the second step. If the goal is an omnichannel view of customers or prospects and their brand interactions, you have to match basic demographic information with device IDs, cookies, online, social, email or mobile handles and behavioral data. There is no industry standard or common tool for doing this well. Add to this challenge the fact that most people have multiple email accounts, divergent social or mobile handles and use different devices for different tasks at different times and you have your analytical work cut out for you.

Segmentation & Hierarchy. Once coherent, robust individual records are created defining segments based on geography, projected life-time value, purchase history or purchase intent, device preference or psycho-demographics will enable a greater ability to provide relevance, utility and value to consumers. Inevitably this requires assigning individuals to each segment and ranking the segments to determine messaging, frequency, cost-of-acquisition and ROI.

Arbitration. Selecting who to talk to, with what message or offer, when and in which channel is the bedrock practical application of Big Data. Pulling the list of likely suspects from the larger data pool requires a series of business rules driven by marketing hypotheses. This usually involves slicing and dicing the data where the sequence of decisions (which data point matters most) will impact the number of names selected.

Big Data offers a big value proposition. But it begins with managing niggly details and complex technical processes that can enable or retard adoption and progress.

5 Data Science Challenges

Data Science is the rage. Agencies and advertisers are scrambling to find analysts and number crunchers to harness the torrent of data spilling out of the web, eCommerce, social and mobile channels.

The promise of aggregating mountains of diverse data from many sources, dicing and slicing them to produce personalized, nuanced, relevant and valuable messages or offers to hundreds of millions of individuals in real time is the customer intimacy fantasy driving the investment and the hype.

Integrating data from multiple channels is considered the only way to get a complete picture of customer interactions, interests and intentions; the missing link for finding the most effective ways to communicate, motivate and capture customer loyalty. The challenge is to make sense of data in ways that personalize the experience for consumers and sell more stuff.

The operative assumption is the richer the data sets, the richer the reward. The underlying marketing conceit is that data mash-ups will yield more personal, relevant and valuable ways to enrich our lives, expand our connections to each other and make our money go further.

The commercial use of data is simultaneously creepy and useful. Studies have shown that the vast majority of Americans will trade off private data for utility or value. As data sets automatically talk to each other, this trade-off will be perceived as less scary and more useful. We are used to being pinged, cued and prompted based on observed or volunteered data.

But the science of data isn't quite that easy. Mobilizing data science in service to brand growth faces these five immediate challenges.

Data Torrent. Forty-five percent of all the data on the planet was generated in the last two years. We are generating data with every breath, click or step. The number of data generation pathways is increasing daily. Collecting, comparing and coordinating data feeds and deciding which data sources are useful and predictive is a big challenge. Marketers have to decide which data points drive business growth and customer satisfaction.

Missing Match Keys. There is no universal data scheme or format. Each data set is constructed on its own. AT&T mobile data is not necessarily connected to a Facebook page or a Gmail account. Individuals leave a trail that marketers can't automatically follow. Even when we collect or aggregate the records we don't necessarily have a common variable to match up the data about an individual.

Multiple Personalities. Matching, profiling and segmenting are further complicated by the fact that individuals have several email or social accounts, multiple mobile devices and endless screen names. Finding any particular person and matching observed, volunteered, purchase history or behavioral data is extremely difficult. Ironically, the old fashioned analog postal address is often the most useful and efficient way to match records or append aggregated data.

Silos. Different organizations and different departments within organizations collect different bits of data, often in different formats, for different purposes. They may or may not talk to each other. More often than not the structures used to house and analyze data are not compatible. Getting a 360-degree portrait of an individual even within a single company is not a slam-dunk.

Privacy. A growing number of people don't want to be profiled, tracked, messaged or engaged. And if they do, they want to do it on *their* terms. Their data is none of your business. They are opting out, complaining to regulators and advocating for stricter data protection policies and laws.

Data and data science are useful and here to stay. Our progress in applying these principles to marketing at scale is still evolving.

Big Data is a Double-Edged Sword

Walgreens is after me. They pursue me day and night using an omnichannel array of technology and messages. They know an awful lot about me and they aren't bashful about using it.

My purchase volume or my margin must be in the top tier or they must be concerned that I might easily defect to CVS or Rite-Aid. Either way their aggressive stance documents the upside and downside of retailers using Big Data for relationship marketing.

There's a Walgreens across the street from my house. They geo fenced me. Every single time I leave the house, I get a text message inviting me into the store. I am one of the 83 million Americans with a Balance Rewards card, which yields a $5 credit for each $100 worth of purchases and countless pre-loaded discounts at the point of sale.

I use the mobile app to renew my medications. They text me, call me at home and work, plus they ping my mobile number with all kinds of reminders. They developed a simple, easy-to-use click-to-reply RX renewal function and they email me frequently to proactively renew my prescriptions. They offer me the option to manage my meds online and they stuff my daily paper with circulars. But somehow nobody ever asked me what I want from the store and nobody ever says "thank you."

They are in my face and all over me, though I'm not sure my present or lifetime value justifies all this attention. Based on the cadence of contact, the multiplicity of channels or the intrusiveness of the messages, they see me as a cornerstone of their business or they so desperately need the transactions they are willing to alienate me in the process.

Ironically, the in-store experience is much less intense. Associates are casual and hard to find. There's always a line because there are never enough cashiers. The pharmacists are a mixed bag, alternately cordial and helpful or snarly.

Walgreens' surround-sound marketing points to the limits of using Big Data aggressively and suggests 3 guidelines for relationship marketers.

Count the Cadence. Brand affinity is impacted by the cumulative sum of brand experiences over time. When customers feel chased or bombarded goodwill is depleted. Brands must understand consumer thinking and consumer routines and then carefully plot when and where interactions make sense. This engagement planning has to be done strictly and solely from the customer perspective. Too many brands, reveling in the number of available touchpoints, carpet bomb customers into submission or attrition.

Ask for Preferences. Everyone likes to be asked what he or she wants and when or how they want it. Brands that solicit preferences and then deliver on them always score higher on awareness, preference and conversion measures. Don't assume or infer that access, downloads or even frequent use of channels or functionalities is an implied preference. Ask.

Balance Utility with Humility. Not worrying about prescriptions is a very useful timesaving benefit. But the incessant number of messages or the sense of being harassed by a low-involvement brand can easily offset the value of this benefit.

A pharmacy is a utility. How much of a deep personal relationship does the average consumer need from a national chain? Face it. The average American wants to get things quickly and easily, avoid a battle over insurance reimbursement, find a good selection of merchandise, get the best deals or prices and then get in and get out. Focus on the basics. Don't pretend to be BFFs. Say please and thank you often.

The agile use of data and evolving digital functionality is a double-edge sword. Skillful use of these tools yields customer loyalty and delight. Presumptive messaging, aggressive pursuit and a never-ending cadence can drive away business and dissipate brand loyalty or preference.

Clairvoyant Marketing

Clairvoyant marketing is a process of collecting "customer data across every touchpoint, supported by real-time analytics to understand and anticipate the experiences that will delight customers." This term, coined at SapientRazorfish, expresses the soon-to-be-routine use of data—in the moment—to proactively engage and delight customers and clients.

By using the data we collect in multiple channels and by understanding the customer experience with brands and the customer journey to and beyond purchase, we can anticipate needs, predict logical and emotional next steps and give customers what they want and what they need even before they know they want it or ask for it.

Clairvoyance rests on the well documented understanding that consumers trade data willingly for relevant access, offers and deals. The combination of personalization, Big Data and on-demand thinking builds an intimate relationship where personal and relevant interactions lead to mutual satisfaction, longevity and brand advocacy. Becoming clairvoyant is a big -- but doable -- ask, which will soon become table stakes for competitive brands.

Here are the building blocks.

Focus on WiiFM. Put yourself in your customers' shoes. Regularly ask "what's in it for me?" A robust brand relationship is a continuous two-way flow of goodwill. What will it take to make your clientele happy? What will it take to make customers feel valued or recognized? How often can they offer advice, ideas and feedback? Merchandise and back-sell the added value. Remind them what's in it for them and what goodies lie ahead.

Anticipate the Next Thing. Map customer journeys to purchase or engagement histories, and figure out the next logical thing. What's the upsell or cross-sell? If they bought X, what is the product cognate or what is the accompanying accessory? What incentives can you offer to continue the journey or enable your consumer to refer friends, share the experience or become a brand advocate?

Understand D-I-Y vs DiFM. In every category there's a Spotify (curated by each individual) and a Pandora (curated by crowdsourcing or by professionals). Offer your customers both options. Then respond in-kind. Use data to suggest products or services similar to those they've selected and create ways for customers to share individual selections and their opinions with others.

Be Realistic. Relationships are built in discrete increments—step-by-step. Anticipate them. Use data to make offers that have a strong propensity to be accepted. Address each segment on its own terms. Craft relevant offers for each segment that account for seasonality, price, volume and fashion. Be practical about timing and frequency of interaction or purchase. Factor in social and mobile technologies.

Purge Friction. Consumers act quickly. They abandon you at the first stumbling block. Examine your process, your sequences and your customer service operation step-by-step. Mystery shop your own brand. Eliminate anything that is confusing or that slows down easy or intuitive access.

Ask Explicitly. Just because you do the math doesn't mean your clients will get the message. After you've crunched the numbers, ask for the order. Be directive. Develop large, colorful explicit response devices. Don't squander the data-driven insight by being reticent.

Make it Someone's Job. Aspirations die without resources. Assign someone to be your customer advocate, charged with responsibly using data, finding patterns and opportunities in customer behavior and protecting consumer privacy. Clairvoyance is a by-product of a skilled analysis that yields insights. The data doesn't matter if you can't find and act on the patterns they reveal.

The brands that become clairvoyant will see greater growth and greater brand loyalty. Brands that embrace data gathering and real time analytic processing will enable intimacy, relevance and advocacy.

AI: A Reality Check

Artificial Intelligence (AI) is the new black, the shiny new object, the answer to every marketer's prayers, and the end of creativity. The recent emergence of AI from the arcane halls of academia and the backrooms of data science has been prompted by stories of drones, robots and driverless cars, undertaken by tech giants like Amazon, Google and Tesla. But the hype exceeds the day-to-day reality.

AI has a fifty-year history of mathematical and computer science development, experimentation and thought. It's not an overnight sensation. What makes it exciting is the confluence of large data sets, improved platforms and software, faster and more robust processing capabilities and a growing cadre of data scientists eager to exploit a wider range of applications. The prosaic day-to-day uses of artificial intelligence and machine learning will make a bigger difference in the lives of consumers and brands than the flashy applications touted in the press.

So consider this AI reality check:

Big Data is Messy. We are creating data and connecting Big Data sets at extraordinary rates, which are multiplying each year. The growth of mobile media, social networks, apps, automated personal assistants, wearables, electronic medical records, self-reporting cars and appliances and the forthcoming Internet of Things (IoT) create enormous opportunities and challenges. In most cases, there is considerable and lengthy work to align, normalize, fill in and connect disparate data long before any analysis can be started.

Collecting, storing, filtering and connecting these bits and bytes to any given individual can be tricky and intrusive. Compiling a so-called "Golden Record" requires considerable computing power, a robust platform, fuzzy logic or deep learning to link disparate pieces of data and appropriate privacy protections. It also requires considerable skill in modeling, and a cadre of data scientists, capable of seeing the forest rather than the trees.

One-to-One is Still Aspirational. The dream of one-to-one personalized communication is on the horizon, but it's still aspirational. The gating factors are the need to develop common protocols for identity resolution, privacy protections, an understanding of individual sensibilities and permissions, the identification of inflection points and a detailed plot of how individual consumers and segments move through time and space in their journey from need to brand preference.

Using AI, we are in an early test-and-learn phase led by companies in the financial services, telecom and retail sectors.

People Prize Predictive Analytics. Amazon trained us to expect personalized recommendations. We grew up online with the notion, "if you liked this, you'll probably like that." As a result, we expect favorite brands to know us and to responsibly use the data we share, knowingly and unknowingly, to make our lives easier, more convenient and better. For consumers, predictive analytics works if the content is personally relevant, useful and perceived as valuable. Anything short of that is SPAM.

But making realistic, practical data-driven predictions is still more art than science. Humans are creatures of habit with some predictable patterns of interest and behavior. But we are not necessarily rational. We are frequently inconsistent, quick to change our minds or course of action, and generally idiosyncratic. AI—using deep learning techniques where the algorithm trains itself—can go some of the way to making sense of this data by monitoring actions over time, aligning behaviors with observable benchmarks and assessing anomalies.

Platform Proliferation. It seems that every tech company is now in the AI space, making all manner of claims. With more than 3500 MarTech offerings, on top of countless installed legacy systems, it's no wonder marketers are confused and IT guys are stymied. A recent *Conductor* survey revealed that 38 percent of marketers surveyed were using 6-10 MarTech solutions and another 20 percent were using 10-20 solutions. Cobbling together a coherent IT landscape in service to marketing objectives, finessing the limitation of legacy systems and existing software licenses while processing massive data sets isn't for the faint of heart. In some cases, AI needs to work around installed technology platforms.

Artificial Intelligence is valuable and evolving. It's not a silver bullet. It requires a combination of skilled data scientists and a powerful contemporary platform directed by a customer-centric perspective and a test-and-learn mentality. Operated in this fashion, AI will deliver much more value to consumers than drones or robots.

Marketing Tech Choices Make a Critical Difference

MAdTech, the combined use of marketing and advertising technologies, is bringing supply chain discipline and a new focus on speed and throughput to the world of Mad Men.

The availability of huge, real time multidimensional data sets and the emergence and refinement of tools to collect, syndicate, schedule, buy, automate or report on marketing communications is forcing marketers to rethink go-to-market strategies and re-engineer production plans and customer engagement processes.

It's no longer just about ideas, offers, words and images. It's about using a vast array of information to make those ideas, offers, words and images matter to your target customers. If you are not assembling your technology ecosystem, you are already behind the eight ball.

Digital, mobile and social marketers have changed the game. Marketing is a 24/7/365 game. Deploying technology is a critical step in service to engaging the right customer at the right time in the right channel. Technology demands that marketers use the right tone of voice and/or the right creative execution to persuasively communicate personal, relevant, useful and entertaining information or offers.

Technology mirrors and interacts with key inflection points in your customers' journey. The savvy players are constructing technology stacks and connecting the pipes to test hypotheses, develop a 360-degree view of their customers and to continuously read results and optimize their marketing tactics. Here are some of the component technologies under consideration.

MDB. A Marketing Database (MDB) is table stakes. Designing a scalable database, capable of aggregating data from many sources and compiling or matching data from diverse sources at the individual record level, is the critical building block for serious customer interaction and engagement. This requires a forward-thinking strategy to understand what data you currently have or can get, what data elements will be available in the near and mid-term, and which data sets will help determine best customers, brand advocates or product and channel preference.

Data Sources. The ability to access, analyze and weight data from many sources will separate the winners from the also-rans. Social, mobile, geographic, ownership, credit and psycho-demographic data is widely available now. Behavioral data from search, web, social, POS, apps and mobile is becoming increasingly available. Being able to map new data to the customers you have (and to their purchase histories) will create the basis for personal, relevant and productive interactions.

BI & Reporting Tools. This software sits on top of a database and enables dicing, slicing and analysis or reporting. These tools make sense of Big Data and help find the insights that drive brand or competitive differentiation. There are many options. Most require sophisticated IT and data science resources to determine the best program for your brand and to extract the most value from this investment.

DMP. Data Management Platforms (DMPs) come in a variety of flavors. All seek to aggregate and represent data in ways that enable segmentation and agile communications. Most require investments in technology and people. There will be intense competition and an endless battle of innovations and improvements among providers for the foreseeable future.

DSP. Demand Side Platforms (DSPs) for programmatic buying is the on-ramp to the media marketplace. DSPs are effective for efficiently buying search, social, mobile, digital display and in-app advertising. This hyper-speed real-time auction model will extend to broadcast and ultimately consume more than half of all buying decisions. Mastering this world, akin to program trading on Wall Street, is difficult because the bogey changes almost daily. A nanosecond can make a significant difference.

MAPs. (Marketing Automation Platforms) Segmentation, triggered messaging and the ability to respond to customers in real time requires an automation tool set. For many agencies and marketers, an alliance with Adobe, Oracle or Marketo is a necessity. The ability to extract data and creative on the fly and the ability to anticipate and pre-program responses to the most likely and most frequent scenarios are becoming baseline expectations. These tools, which are getting increasingly sophisticated, enable brands to cement intimate relationships.

Content Tools. Collecting, editing, storing and distributing content in written, graphic, audio, video and AR/VR formats is becoming a requirement for efficient marketing. Content management tools, multi-channel scheduling applications and secure storage capabilities allow marketers to squeeze maximum value from every hour or dollar invested in the creative process. For larger brands, these tools facilitate widespread use and adaptation across geographies or customer segments.

Ultimately, marketing technology infrastructure is a determinant of marketing success. The time is now to assess resources, assemble or reassemble your technology landscape and put the right architecture in place for downrange success.

You Are Your MarTech Stack

Winning attention, engagement and loyalty with today's consumers requires an automated agile marketing infrastructure. MarTech choices are many, noisy and highly competitive. But to succeed in engaging mobile, social and increasingly digital consumers, you are your MarTech stack.

Marketing technology impacts inflection points in the customer journey. Savvy players are constructing technology stacks to test hypotheses, develop a 360-degree view of their customers and to continuously optimize tactics.

Here are the critical considerations.

D-I-Y vs DiFM? The key decision involves choices about cost, resources and IT integration. One-size-fits-all solutions from the likes of Adobe, Oracle or Salesforce pre-package functionalities and offer the promise of frictionless throughput, even though most of these offerings have been cobbled together through acquisition. It's a Do it For Me (DiFM), one throat to choke solution that gives you speed to market and someone to blame.

The alternative is to Do It Yourself (D-I-Y) by custom assembling the pieces and parts of a MarTech landscape, selecting best-in-class elements, and investing in software development to stitch them together. This requires time, expertise, patience and internal alignment on what is necessary, what is nice to have, and what is affordable.

The hybrid approach—go the pre-packaged route but customize it—adds selected functionality or software onto top of pre-packaged solutions to meet specific needs, but requires a willing partner and a considerable investment in developers. It can be costly, technically complex and requires skilled project managers.

Data Storage. Step two is finding the right approach to collect, clean and store data from multiple and multiplying sources. Choosing the appropriate and scalable marketing database (MDB) or a data management platform (DMP), both equivalent of a digital filing cabinet, requires an understanding and a forward-looking projection of what data is available and useful now, and which supplemental data elements might be added to enhance customer profiles or derive added insights in the future. The decision frequently locks data into a schema which can be hard to change or expand and difficult to migrate as new products and approaches come on line.

Data Insight. On top of a storage solution marketers need tools to connect, mine and correlate data elements in ways that deliver insight and lead to actionable marketing tactics. Tools must be agile enough to combine and compare data elements in real time and over longer time periods. They are critical enablers of robust customer profiles and should be capable of linking disparate data points from many sources. Ideally the toolset should be able to create data signals that are reusable and can be combined or recombined on demand to suit campaign or brand challenges. Most require sophisticated IT and data science resources to determine the best program for your brand and to extract the most value from this investment.

Data Deployment. Delivery of branded messaging across channels requires sophisticated deployment tools especially in light of changes in email, mobile and social usage patterns. In addition, segmentation, personalization, triggered messaging and the ability to respond to customers in real time requires automated tools. For many, an alliance with Adobe, Oracle, Salesforce or Marketo is a necessity and competitive table stakes.

Data Reporting & Visualization. Increasingly, data and the results of data-driven insights need to be shared and analyzed by non-specialists. This necessitates tools to display, relate and simplify complexities or illuminate nuances into terms or images that can prompt action. Tableau and Domo have captured the imagination of many marketers eager to create management dashboards that get more than a passing glance. More than pretty pictures, these tools lay bare campaign performance, message resonance, key segments, competitive inroads or brand vulnerabilities that need to be understood and addressed.

The critical criteria for choosing an automation, ESP or DSP partner is the ability to extract data and creative on the fly and the ability to anticipate and pre-program responses to the most likely and most frequent scenarios. Consumers are conscious of the data they have given up and expect marketers to know them by using their data to deliver relevant, useful and valuable content. These tools enable brands to cement intimate customer relationships.

Ultimately the MarTech stack determines marketing success. The time is now to assess resources, assemble or reassemble your technology landscape and put the right architecture in place for future success.

The Human Side of Big Data

Big Data is about human relationships. If advertising is art in service of commerce, Big Data is math in service to relationships. The fundamental underlying concept is the better you know someone, the more relevant, useful and valuable the message and the connection can be. Data science exists to try to duplicate the collection, sorting, weighing and application of information that drive friendships.

Here are the relationship assumptions and human behavior patterns that inform complex computations and the application of marketing technology. Rather than think of Big Data as a scary invasive "big brother," think of it as a mechanism for ensuring that the right people get the right message when they are engaged and ready to act. One potentially depressing reality, demonstrated by the use of Big Data, is that we are not unique and much more predictable than we think we are.

Birds of feather flock together. Like-minded people seek each other out. This is a pattern infused deep in our limbic brains and reinforced by cultural and ethnic orientation. We stick to people who are like us and share our backgrounds, education and income. Most consumers can be found and categorized by their zip code. So by pinpointing target customers by geography, class and ethnicity, marketers can make fundamental assumptions about wants, needs and preferences.

Demographics are Destiny. The apple doesn't fall far from the tree. We are products of genetics, early experience, education and familial behavior patterns. We are essentially an amalgam of whom we came from. And while some people make a radical break with their past and many of us re-invent ourselves in unique and interesting ways, we are, for the most part, reflections of our psycho-demographics. So marketers, understanding who we are, can apply this data to what we want, what we do, where we go and what we care about. If they do it right, we get information that's valuable; if not, we are annoyed.

We are creatures of habit and patterns. Everyone filters, sorts and prioritizes the countless stimuli we receive each day. Most of this process is unconscious. But each person determines the things we like, the things that give us comfort, the things that reflect our self-esteem, the stuff we hate or the status we'd like to have. We build a series of preferences and coping mechanisms to make sense of the blooming, buzzing noisy world around us.

In doing so, we leave identifiable patterns, many of which are similar to people like us. These patterns and repeat actions are discoverable and, to some extent, predictable, using algorithms. So brands mine Big Data to identify patterns and document the behaviors and attitudes represented by these patterns.

Change is Challenging. Inertia is the Universal Competitor. Most of us operate in comfortable daily circumstances and repeat all kinds of patterns. Our default behavior is to do nothing. We shop at the same places, eat at the same restaurants, vacation in the same spots, drive the same routes and, in general, vary marginally from practical, familiar and safe routines. Changing something big—a hairstyle, a car, a sports fandom, a house or a spouse—is a huge challenge, frequently upsetting an otherwise settled life.

Marketers use this information to determine who to address and how to address them using Big Data. There are predictive variables that separate people with a propensity to change or switch from those that won't. Ideally this improves the relevance and resonance of the messages each person receives.

People Buy Into Brands. Americans don't just buy stuff. They identify with the brands that reflect their interests, needs and sensibilities. Consumers buy into brands rather than just buy them off the shelf. Conversely, brands are designed to appeal to specific cohorts with specific interests and characteristics. These affiliations, both attitudinal and behavioral, are routinely tracked and used in targeting campaigns.

Because people buy into brands and willingly give up personal data to get information, content, deals and offers, they expect their favorite brands to know them and use the data volunteered to personalize their experience and super serve their needs. Mercenary shoppers armed with a what's-in-it-for-me mentality (WiiFM) expect their favorite brands to know them and act accordingly by doing-it-for-me (DiFM) and delivering messages that are personally relevant, useful and valuable. Collecting, processing and using Big Data sets enable and improve ongoing relationships.

RFM Rules. When we do something—like signing up, viewing a video or buying something—we are much more likely to do it again, sooner rather than later. This notion of recency and frequency powers most loyalty and reward programs. Someone taking a given action is 10 times more likely to do it again than the average person.

The choices people make, the brands they select, the stores they visit and the goods and services they buy can be tracked, categorized and revisited by marketers. It's not an accident that when you make a charitable donation or an important purchase you hear from the brand soon after.

Big Data sounds much scarier than it is. Used legally, properly and respectfully by ethical and conscientious marketers, it can make consumers' lives easier, less cluttered and more convenient.

Practice Partial Personalization

Personalized communication prompts better, faster and deeper response and engagement. But few marketers have mastered the ability to personalize messages and many more are reluctant to try it.

In surveys conducted by Demand Metric and Seismic, the leading reasons for not personalizing messaging were lack of technology, bandwidth and data. The stumbling blocks seem to be anxiety about the use of data, access or use of technology and resistance to the idea of customized creative.

On one hand, appending a first and/or last name to an otherwise generic message is superficial, hardly enough personalization to spike response or engagement. And while personally identifiable information is needed to achieve genuine one-to-one communications, using multiple timely personal details can easily freak out consumers and aggravate anxieties about privacy. Similarly, triggered messaging based on behavior can be a double-edged sword. Some consumers will appreciate a follow-up or a reminder. Others will be annoyed.

The middle ground is to segment the audience and use group-level affiliations to make a partially personal connection. By referencing an interest, a vertical industry issue, geography, job title or list source, marketers can reduce the distance between brands and their customers or prospects. Each individual will understand and process these references as they relate directly to themselves. The net impact will be to signal a higher level of interest, recognition and understanding between brands and their people.

The reluctance to use partial personalization seems to lie in the belief that the cost and the mechanics of limited customization aren't worth the result. Yet, there is significant evidence that relevance, utility and value unlock customer relationships and drive business and loyalty. By adding easily recognizable touch points, brands can improve response and engagement at modest costs.

From a creative and production perspective, partially personalizing email, text messages, video and direct mail is reasonably easy at affordable costs. New technologies and upgraded CMS platforms make it simple to shuffle creative modules and/or infuse unique copy or data into otherwise generic formats.

Partial personalization trumps superficial salutations and sidesteps the creepy privacy implications of extensive use of Big Data. Brands can access data and personalization tools as services and ought to be testing them.

My friend and former client, Bert Shlensky, president of startupconnection.com, put it this way: "The more you can make someone feel valued like an individual, the more they are going to prefer you over the place next door. At the end of the day, dealing with people on a personal level is the key to creating relationships and building loyalty that can last for decades."

One-to-One Media Plans on the Horizon

Real one-to-one marketing, an idea evangelized by Peppers & Rogers in the mid-90s, is finally on the horizon. The availability and confluence of psycho-demographic, mobile, digital, social and retail data will soon enable marketers to know definitively what every individual likes, does and wants in order to craft individual media plans.

Connecting and combining Big Data sets with high capacity, fast-processing servers will enable marketers to get more granular than ever. The implication is that media will no longer be a tapestry of channels, aimed at broad segments, like "Soccer Moms" or "vegans." Instead, media plans will be constructed to reach and persuade each "Soccer Mom" or "vegan," one-by-one.

The confluence of data comes from several sources, each of which aggregates, combines, compares, models and rents data.

Traditional Data Compilers. These Big Data houses have hundreds of data points on virtually every American above the age of 18. From driver's license to age, income, education, device ownership, zip code or interests, the variables can be matched and married to a postal or email address and, increasingly, to a mobile phone number. Data co-ops put purchase histories and retail offers into the marketplace where they can be matched with many other data points. The Big Data houses know who you are, what you do and like, and where to find you.

ESPs. Email Service Providers, especially the big ones, transmit billions of emails and keep track of everyone. They know which brands sent each offer to every discrete list. They also know who opened, clicked or bounced. Combining email behavior with traditional psycho-demographic data validates segmentations and inferences as it enables finer filtering, targeting and retargeting.

DSPs. Demand Side Platforms track ads served and retargeted online. Amassing huge cookie pools, these tools track millions of individuals, keystroke-by-keystroke, revealing what you looked at and when, what you clicked on in sequence and how you interacted online. This data reveals personal patterns, likes and repeat visits as well as affinities shared with like-minded people.

Mobile Phone Companies. These guys track, compile and merchandise phone use. They know which device is in use, when, for how long and where. They have a stored history of use and can model past activities or project likely future behavior.

SDKs. Software Development Kits are the fundamental building blocks of apps. This software natively tracks every open and click, records usage patterns, scores and, in some cases, can map sequential app usage. This data reveals how individuals spend their time, what they do, how often and with what results.

Imagine brands combining these data sources into a massive data mart and using this robust information to build look-alike, propensity, logistic regression and churn models and you have the reasonable probability of categorizing and mapping millions of individual behaviors. Feed this data into a marketing automation system driven by a set of business rules, triggered by if/then data points or sophisticated models and algorithms, and you are perfectly poised to get up close and personal.

The trick will be to ensure that all this fancy math and sophisticated technology yields messaging or offers that are genuinely personal, relevant and useful.

This level of granularity and interaction scares many and triggers privacy concerns. But time and time again, consumers have indicated a willingness to trade data and suffer unprovoked interactions in return for things they care about or offers that resonate.

The objective of applying Big Data and data science to marketing is two-fold: to better understand customers and improve the customer experience by reducing annoying irrelevant interruptions and to create compelling, relevant communication, targeted to the right people, at the right moment, in their preferred channel. Leveraging data to accomplish these twin goals will get us to the ability to create and execute individual media plans.

Why Mad Men Aren't Embracing Math Men

Big Data is the new marketing darling. Yet mainstream marketers haven't been walking the walk. Very few Mad Men have become Math Men.

Some industries have to be data-centric marketers because their margins and share of wallet demand it. Yet even in these firms, data lives in silos and lacks integrated analytics necessary to significantly impact business growth. For example, in retail and grocery, we've been playing around with purchase histories, private label credit cards, web analytics, social media, mobile use patterns and loyalty programs, but very few marketers truly integrate multi-channel data, build impactful data marts or fully exploit the power in the data.

So how can rational competitive marketers utilize a growing, robust suite of tools that could make them smarter, faster and richer? Here are 6 things we need to overcome.

Math Phobia. Most of us suck at math. Couple this with the feeling that math constrains creativity and you have an attitudinal bias against using the data at hand. Marketers have to get over this basic hurdle.

Talent Deficit. The really good math guys don't work in marketing or advertising. Agencies, marketers, e-merchants and publishers are constantly trolling for hard-to-find analysts, database administrators and database marketers and coming up short. For real math savants, advertising is baby stuff. Fortunately, there are alliances to be made with data shops and Watson to consider.

Low IT Priority. Database projects are low priority for corporate IT leaders. Marketing needs are perceived to be far below complex, big budget aspirational IT landscape, software or architecture projects. Marketing data applications tend to require much more hands-on technical support and service because marketers are unwilling or unable to run the software themselves. So IT guys run the other way. Successful brands will get executive management to make Big Data an IT priority.

Impact Perceptions. The technology is much more complex and confusing than making ads or building websites, and because it's perceived as plumbing, data investments can be cut, delayed or ignored without fear of harming business results. Ironically, the truth is exactly the opposite. By strategically investing in plumbing and crunching the numbers you can add substantial value quickly and predictably. An investment of X will pay out 10X in a time frame that would surprise everyone.

Data Overload. Brands collect mountains of data and create colorful dashboards they can't make sense of. Don't be willing to trade off customer insight, segmentation, personalization or customer intimacy because there are too many numbers. Focus on the indicators that can drive business.

Big Brother. Fear of violating privacy rules limit Big Data adoption. The reality is we have pretty good transparent consumer privacy laws, none of which has dampened consumers' willingness to trade their personal data for deeper deals and relationships.

The effective use of Big Data can drive engagement, intimacy and customer satisfaction without becoming Big Brother. The number and sophistication of data sets and the tools to use them are growing daily. Mad Men need to embrace, adopt, ally or marry Math Men to remain relevant and competitive.

SECTION IV

EMAIL

Email's 10 Commandments

To optimize email marketing, you need to stand out from the loud, growing and frequent crowd and take concerted action to get attention for your brand and your message.

Start with the end. What do you want the recipients of your email to feel, think or do? If this is a one-off effort it will need to work differently than if it's part of a newsletter, club or continuity program. Clarity on the front end will make measurement and analysis much easier on the back end

Create a distinctive look or feel. Experiment with subject lines and with Personal URL's in the subject line. Use the same template or color palette and be sure it instantly cues brand recognition. People trust the FROM line so don't get cute; use your brand.

Build a Consistent Delivery Schedule. Train your customers to expect certain messages at certain times (Tuesday = Bargain day). Consider a value-oriented TO address to reinforce the content or the value implicit in a consistent series of offers.

Segment and Target Customers. Test the criteria that suit your marketing objective. Communicate the criteria in the subject line. Be sure the value-add is immediately and clearly apparent in the subject line. Don't exceed 40 characters.

Send Less Better. Rather than do one blast of a million names, do 5 blasts of 200,000 names. Make each segment a different offer or relate the offer to something you know about the behavior of customers in that segment. Focus on behavior; it's the only reliable predictor of future action.

Work on the List. Every list is flawed. Names carefully opted-in by brand loyalists will perform much better than random names gathered by lead generation sites or list compilers. Use list cleaning, merge/purge and integrity tools. Negotiate a "net name" deal.

RFM Rules. Peg email blasts to frequency of action. People who take a desired action are much more likely to do it again and much sooner than someone who opted in, but rarely responds.

Tighten the Content. Short directive copy works best because everyone scans and nobody reads. Many emails are read without fully opening the browser frame or on mobile devices. Load the core idea and the offer into the opening paragraph and the pre-header.

Limit Response Options. Customers or prospects should be given a limited number of response choices. The more choices you offer, the less response you get. One big button high up works best.

Be CAN SPAM compliant. Every legit email has to show who it came from, including a postal address, and offer an opt-out mechanism. There is absolutely nothing worse than being a spammer.

5 Clues for Improving Email Impact

Email is the principal channel connecting brands and consumers. Everyone uses email. In surveys conducted by MarketingSherpa, 91 percent of adults polled liked receiving promotional emails and 7 in 10 prefer email as the channel for communication with brands. But until recently, we didn't know much about the patterns of personal email use and the texture of email interactions and conversations--data that can potentially help make branded email more relevant, personal and impactful.

Researchers from Yahoo Labs and the USC Information Sciences Institute analyzed 16 billion emails exchanged on Yahoo Mail among and between 2 million anonymous people in an attempt to understand what drives response and what prolongs or dissolves email conversations. Their report, titled "Evolution of Conversations in the Age of Email Overload," is our first broad peek into how email conversations really play out.

Here's what they found:

Reply is a function of volume. The more email you get, the more you try to respond to. Users send and reply to more emails as their inbox volume increases. But as the volume grows, the percentage of response decreases. As you might imagine, inbox overload affects older adults differently than younger people. They get overwhelmed easier and faster.

Speed is Expected. Email implies fast interactions. The most likely reply time is two minutes. Half of all replies studied were responded to within 47 minutes of receipt. Ninety percent of email replies happen within a day of receiving a message. Given an expectation of immediacy and urgency, many of the responses mirror the length and the language of the original.

Device Matters. Consumers reply to emails sent from smartphones almost twice as fast as from tablets (28 minutes versus 57 minutes) or desktops (28 minutes versus 62 minutes). Similarly, the length of replies varies by device. Smartphones prompt short replies of 20 words or less. Tablet replies increase to 27 words and desktop replies reach a loquacious level of 60 words. All age groups have embraced mobile devices for sending and receiving email. Women have a slight edge in this regard.

Timing Affects Response. The content of email received during the workweek is significantly longer than those received on weekends. Perhaps people see email as intrusive of their non-working time. But response times are shorter Monday through Friday. Copy length varies by time of day. From 9am 'til 11pm reply time is the shortest. Early morning email has the longest reply time.

Age Counts. Teens are cryptic in their use of email. They write short messages and reply quickly. In contrast, older adults still remember letter writing and write longer messages and more thoughtful responses.

And while email is broadly valued and preferred, keep in mind that most people are looking to sort, filter and eliminate emails, not necessarily open and click on them. Interaction is a function of brand trust, perceived value and reduced anxiety. In context, these findings suggest five clear directions for marketers to improve email resonance and response:

Assume Mobile Reception. Structure the templates and the copy for mobile use. Bake in short sequential messages and easy-to-use reply buttons. Anticipate broad use of smartphones, which should yield the fastest replies. Be sure to capitalize on the consumer expectation of urgency.

Telegraph the Message. Create short, punchy clear messages with prominent calls to action and easy-to-use buttons. Make your point succinctly and direct the receiver to respond immediately.

Anticipate Interaction. Back-and-forth patterns yield the best relationships. Create a sequence of messages, not just a solo blast. Expect a dialogue to transpire even if your part of it is automated. Very few productive conversations are one-and-done. Plan the logical sequences and engage customers step-by-step.

Leverage Circadian Rhythms. Consumers are focused on email weekdays from 9am until11pm. Plan your interactions then. Remember that Tuesday and Wednesday mornings yield the most, longest and fastest responses. We are creatures of habit. Intersect and intercept customers doing what they naturally do.

Know Your Audience. Tailor messages by age and device. Give older people more copy and younger people less. Push younger consumers to reply quicker. Plan more elaborate graphic or video creative aimed at desktop, laptop and tablet users.

Peeking into the dynamics of personal email patterns gives us many new clues for improving the timing and impact of branded email campaigns. Aligning a marketing or messaging strategy with native consumer behavior patterns almost always creates incremental value for both parties.

4 New Email Insights

The beautiful thing about email marketers is that they measure everything and frequently share their data. MailerMailer analyzed 1.1 billion emails from 56,000 campaigns run in 33 industries.

Here's my interpretation of their results in four observations.

Mobile Rules. Almost three in every four emails are opened on a mobile device. Smartphone users check their phones 60+ times each day. Mobile open rates are higher than average. Clicks are lower because the phone has become a default boredom avoidance device. Consumers want to know what's coming in but don't necessarily want to engage or interact in the moment.

The implications are: 1. Email must render properly on every mobile OS. 2. Put the most important content first. 3. Make a clear and directive call to action. 4. CTA buttons must be big, bold, colorful and fat-finger friendly.

It's a Speed Round. Email is a fast-acting stimulus-and-response medium. In a typical email transmission, opens peak after the first hour of delivery. Half of the response comes in the first 5 hours after delivery. By 15 hours, three-quarters of all opens will happen, and by 48 hours the game is over with more than 90 percent of all expected response completed.

Context and concise copy matter drive response. Marketers need to time their shots and forecast response in a tighter time frame. Ask yourself, what do I want consumers to think, feel and do and when do I want them to do it? Then plan accordingly. Focus on what people normally want and intercept them in the process of getting it. Edit out anything that doesn't impact fast engagement.

There is evidence that emails sent on Mondays or Fridays between 6pm and 2am drive the biggest open and click rates. People generally open emails in the morning as part of their daily routine and work through them chronologically. Emails that are waiting for them in their inboxes get a 3-4 second scan and sort to determine what gets read and what gets deleted.

Urgency and Deals Drive Opens. Subject lines play a disproportionate role in driving opens. Messages of 28 to 39 characters, medium length, with words signaling offers or deals (free, sale, deals, coupons, newsletter or events) or time sensitive cues (today, this week, weekend, daily) prompted the most opens at 12.6percent, a full point above the previous average open rate of 11.6percent.

Subject Lines are Billboards. They must be simple, clear, immediately understandable and intuitive. And they must instantly communicate what's in it for someone to click. Forget about sophisticated word play, puns, allegory, metaphors, alliteration, clichés or witty turns of phrase. There's nothing subtle or shaded about a subject line. If an eighth grader can't get it in an instant, rewrite the subject line.

Ask Early and Often for Clicks. Click rates have steadily declined over the last few years, probably because consumers aren't engaged or motivated by what they find when they open an email. And while many factors impact click rates, relevance, utility, clarity of messages and directive mechanics are the most important factors.

Many marketers believe that a single call to action yields the most click-throughs. But there is growing evidence that different or multiple CTAs do better. Messages that contained 21 or more links drove click rates of 2.1 percent, a 100 percent increase over messages with 1 to 5 links. This might be a testament to the prevalence of eNewsletters or the widespread use of sale emails with long lists of products and deal options. It also might signal a consumer need for choice and options.

The guys at Behave.org hypothesize that "when it comes to clearly giving your users relevant and distinguishably different choices, more may actually be better." In a recent test where 2 CTAs beat a solo CTA, they made a distinction between actions that require different levels of effort or commitment (e.g. deposit versus play). By "using distinct CTA buttons to get your users to perform different tasks," two sets of consumers can find something to click on. Low commitment or lower friction terms for CTAs or on buttons drive more clicks deeper into the conversion funnel.

Email marketing is a process of continuous measurement, observation and improvement. I hope these observations will add to your optimization efforts.

A New Email Marketing Tactic

Asynchronous triggered mail is intriguing. The idea is that consumer behavior drives email dispatch. So, rather than blast out a million emails to a targeted list on Tuesday morning (the spray and pray approach), you deliver the same million emails one-by-one over the course of a month.

Based on using pixel tracking, brands determine which sites or behaviors are related to their product or service and which actions might infer interest in their brands. They make a buy, much like retargeting on these sites, but rather than trigger a display banner ad or a social media unit, the action triggers an email. Yahoo and Gmail already do a version of this tactic by mining email accounts and triggering text messages and interstitial ads based on the content of the email consumers receive.

Almost half of all email is opened on mobile devices, where conversion is notoriously low. Open rates in general hover around 30 percent. And there is really no optimal day/ time combination to maximize email response. So the idea of adapting email as a one-to-one tool is appealing. Asynchronous delivery, also called email on-demand, has the potential to change the perception of this trusted channel from a mass medium to personalized marketing vehicle.

It's also a way to shift a consumer's attention away from his phone to a larger, more responsive device like his desktop, laptop or tablet. And one-by-one behavior triggered transmission can potentially engage non-openers, cart abandoners or lapsed buyers and reduce the annoyance of email carpet-bombing that retail brands default to in the fourth quarter.

This is an emerging technology that will enhance the value of email and is well worth a test.

SECTION V

MOBILE

Mobility Changes Everything

Mobility is turning everyone into direct, relationship and database marketers. The key to successfully making this transformation will be surrendering control to consumers while continuously creating relevant and resonant content.

Let's start with a few key facts.

Mobile is here. More than half of all Americans have smartphones. Most brand marketers know this but haven't put either strategy or infrastructure in-place. Too many are still arguing about the value of responsive design. Mobility changes almost everything.

Smartphones have replaced PCs, watches, rolodexes, maps, cameras, game devices, remote controls, landlines, books, boarding passes, coupons and loyalty cards. And they are closing in on wallets. People spend as much time with their phones as they do with TV.

Smartphones are an appendage for younger consumers. Their phones are very personal, heavily customized and in constant use. Don't be surprised if Levi's or Lee creates jeans with a special quick-draw phone pocket, which also prevents inadvertent butt dialing.

Apps are "hit" driven. There are millions of them. They rise into and fall out of fashion as quickly as the Top 40. The average person has 40 on their phone, but only really uses 8-10. New research suggests that 5 apps draw 80 percent of all app usage. Getting onto a consumer's phone is tough. Staying on is even tougher. A successful app must either provide instant utility or endless entertainment.

Open beats closed systems. Android is ascendant and will continue to be because it's becoming ubiquitous. Apple may have a few tricks up its sleeve. But my bet's on Android, and its many variations across devices and geographies, to ultimately dominate.

Soon apps and native phone technologies will work together and talk to each other. Think about how interoperability might impact your business. For example, the accelerometer notices you are walking funny and double checks with the pedometer. The GPS pipes up and says you're off course on your way home. The med app then quickly checks your heart rate and blood pressure, and then signals the Walgreen's app to reorder your meds.

Context Matters. Where you are (location) and what you're doing (attention) determine your mood and your openness to brands. Your customer is not the same person when they wake up as when they are working mid-day; each persona has different needs and desires. Understanding creature movement through time and attendant attitudes will give you clues about customer interest and receptivity.

Americans are putting computers in their pockets and expecting them to work and add value on-demand. Brands have to ask themselves, "Are you interrupting them or making life a little better?" To the extent that consumers use your app, you have an always-on virtual private network (VPN) connection to them. You have to respect this and use it sparingly.

Force yourself to provide genuine consistent value while ensuring privacy.

There is great opportunity to claim mind and heart space and an equal opportunity to frustrate, annoy and alienate. When you're in, you're in 'til you blow it. When you're out, you're out for good.

The implications of these facts are staggering and challenging. To harness mobility, master these 5 moves.

Think Differently. Customers demand personalized, relevant attention, designed around their needs and wants rather than around your marketing channels. If you don't change the way you think about engaging these customers, you will quickly lose relevance.

Surrender Control. Interested and loyal customers prefer to drive the relationship. Enable them to set preferences for all aspects of their interactions with the brand. Let them tell you how often they want to hear from, what channels they prefer and which products or services they care about most. Ask permission to use location, purchase history and other data to customize their experiences. Brands that focus on relevance over reach and value over frequency build enduring relationships.

Target Context. Think about lifestyles, life stages, time of day and the customer journey with a UX and a service-oriented mindset. Smartphones and tablets are used to do distinct tasks—check an account, make a payment, find directions, grab a coupon, research a restaurant, compare prices, look up a word or a trivia fact or check product specifications. Figure out what your best customers do, when and where they do it and then map your brand to the things they do or care about.

Most of us are creatures of habit. We have predictable likes and dislikes and identifiable routines and patterns that can cue marketers about what we want. Where can you make things easier, simpler, faster, cheaper or more fun? Then craft content and messaging to deliver them at these critical inflection points.

Marketers need to collect, aggregate and process data to push relevant messages at relevant times or locations to their customers. Well-designed "push" messages deliver increased engagement and brand preference over time.

Don't Sell. Smartphones and tablets are personalized tools. Overt selling, especially offers without opt-ins, are strictly verboten. Brands can deepen the relationship by providing utility, value and content, which, if done right, pre-sells products and services and engenders significantly more awareness, consideration and preference than traditional advertising.

This requires nerves of steel and a bit of faith, especially if you're on the hook for increased revenue or margins. But we are seeing the limits of and a backlash to SMS ads, in-app ads and social ads today.

Selling is about buying into the gestalt, ecosystem, values and personality of a brand. These intangibles are best nurtured with personalized, relevant and useful content as much as with deals, offers and coupons. There's no happier customer than one who gets a pointed, personal message from a brand they love, at the time and through the channel they've chosen, with an offer about something they want.

Make it Easy. People get frustrated with technology in a nanosecond. Invest in user experience and responsive design. Make sure that your assets render and display properly on all devices and that accessing your content, offers and products is easy, intuitive and quick.

People on the move have ridiculously high expectations for instant gratification. When you meet them, you gain a special, but fleeting, moment of love. If you frustrate them, you are over and out. Increasingly, brands are being judged by their ability to deliver what an individual wants on demand. Given where most of us are today, it's a tall order.

Embrace Mobile Marketing

Consumers have embraced mobile devices with a vengeance. Everyone has a mobile device. Everyone has access to a huge percentage of all human knowledge in their back pocket. And everyone expects always on everywhere access to virtually everything.

More than half of all email is opened on a mobile device and a third of eCommerce takes place on either a smartphone or a tablet. Think about these astounding statistics curated by Gravit8:

Americans are Totally Mobile.

- Wireless penetration is at 104 percent in the USA
- 75 percent of those devices are SMS enabled
- 91 percent of the US population has a mobile device within reach 24/7
- Americans spend an average of 2 hours and 57 minutes each day on a smartphone or tablet—more time than watching TV

Text Messages are Commercially Acceptable.

- Over 90 percent of text messages are read in the first 3 minutes after receipt
- Text messages have a response rate 20 times greater than email or direct mail
- 64 percent of those who've subscribed to mobile marketing messages made a purchase as a result

Mobile Search Drives Purchases.

- Consumers send 15+ hours/week researching online using smartphones
- Mobile searchers visit a website, on average, six times
- 93 percent of those searching on mobile devices complete a purchase

To anticipate and proactively serve the growing expectations of mobile users, we have to rethink mobile marketing and engagement tactics.

Build an Opt-In List. Brands have been skittish about asking for mobile opt-ins. Fearful that mobile is the last bastion of consumer privacy, brands have not aggressively sought or incented consumer opt-ins. Evidently this taboo is overstated. Start asking for mobile numbers and start building your list. Connect mobile numbers with existing data to create robust segments and enable micro-targeting.

Develop Use Cases. If we have the devices at hand 24/7, plot out what we are doing, where we are going and what we are thinking or feeling. Then craft experiences and messages to intersect our moods and our movements through time and space. The widespread use of mobile devices offers brands a virtual VPN to customers. Once you are in their pockets, if you can get in their heads and track them through the day, you can potentially create intense and loyal relationships, assuming brands can create relevant, personal and valuable content or offers.

Be Spontaneous. Text messaging is an immediate and reflexive response device. It's well suited to spur of the moment offers, games and quick polls or surveys. It's also a great way to time announcements or seek instant feedback. Think about how your brand can leverage the technology, the unique beeping sounds and the expectation of immediate back-and-forth to surprise or delight customers.

Focus on Search. A huge number of users search first. Licensing a robust mobile search tool that can be geo-targeted, can store user search history and maybe even predict searches based on past use are worth the expense. Embed offers in search terms and develop dedicated mobile landing pages to capitalize on the purchasing tailwind that search provides.

Zero-In on Device Usage. Consumers are turning to specific devices to accomplish specific things. Smartphones are the all-purpose in-motion utility device. Tablets are becoming multi-dimensional infotainment centers. Keep an eye on these behaviors. Create content, manage messaging and produce promotions using native functionality to leverage existing device usage and provide consumers with an experience that will feel natural, organic, useful and fun.

If you're not mobile, you're standing still or falling behind. That's the clear implication. Either you're embracing increased consumer mobility and the continuing evolution of mobile devices or you're road kill on the information superhighway.

For Mobile Engagement ... Speed Counts

In life, timing is everything. Timing—expressed as speed, intuitive content and instant perception of value or utility– are the critical variables for successfully engaging consumers on mobile devices.

Research by Facebook, Twitter and others document a different pace of information flow and information processing on mobile devices. Information flows to smartphones and tablets quickly and in discrete bytes. Three out of four people have their phones constantly with them. Users typically look at their phones 30+ times each day and quickly scroll through the latest messages.

By definition it's a quick-look, fast-paced environment. Think about your own behavior. You're online scrolling through emails or texts instantly separating out real people from subscriptions or offers. You click several, then immediately back out looking for the next thing. You absorb a fair amount of information just from the headlines. Or you click on a video and watch the first few seconds to decide if it's worth a further investment of your time. Opens are strong. Click-throughs are not.

Twitter used eye tracking to discover that people consume content faster on mobile devices. Facebook found that mobile users consume content in 1.7 seconds versus 2.5 seconds on desktop machines. Recall is also faster—as quickly as a single second, according to research done by Fors-Marsh. These findings were mirrored by Nielsen for Twitter, which found significant video recall after only one second of viewing.

One example is mobile coupon redemption. Sixty-five percent of mobile coupons are redeemed within five minutes of seeing it, according to a study of 104 million coupon users by Koupon Media. This quick recognition and conversion cycle makes the case for processing speed. It is enhanced by context; coupons are often geo-targeted and increasingly triggered in-store. This fast-paced attention-action sequence will become the norm, especially with younger audiences.

Viewed from the opposite perspective, Retale found that consumers have little tolerance for accidently clicked ads. Many people inadvertently click on ads and within milliseconds back out and are annoyed, frustrated or angry. Instant awareness of content prompts fast, almost immediate, action.

Brand marketers have to factor in context and assume quick, divided attention for mobile messages and plan accordingly. Here are 7 creative implications:

1. You need an arresting hook to grab consumer attention.
2. Subject lines and headlines must be telegraphic.
3. Product or personalities must capture attention in seconds.
4. Journalism's inverted pyramid should drive content creation—headline, RTBs, details.
5. Communicate relevance, utility and/or value instantly.
6. Content must sell-in each sequential second.
7. Calls to action must be big, colorful and prominent.

Consumers are in motion. Increased use of more powerful and sophisticated devices by all psycho-demographic segments is a given. Activating customers or prospects as they move through time and space, not to mention as they consider your brand, is a speed round. Strip away all extra rhetoric. Present your case quickly and clearly.

Building the Next Killer App

With billions of apps in use—the majority of which are deleted within the first six months after they're downloaded—we are beginning to understand consumer expectations, usage patterns and segmentation to guide the next round of app development.

Eighty-eight percent of the 177 minutes Americans spend watching video each day takes place on smartphones or tablets. Nineteen percent of older adults (65+) are watching TV on mobile devices. Mobile use outpaces TV watching. The average person touches his or her smartphone 150 times each day. Seventy-one percent of Bank of America survey respondents admitted to sleeping with their smartphone. Millions more check their phone first thing every morning.

The average user spends 30 hours and 15 minutes using apps each month. He or she checks a mobile app every six minutes. So called "mobile addicts," who number 280 million people, according to Flurry, launch apps more than 60 times each day. Consumers use apps 6 times more frequently than websites. According to Compuware, 80 percent of consumers prefer mobile apps to traditional websites and 79 percent make purchase decisions based on using a mobile device, half within one hour of use.

Social and messaging apps, utilities and productivity apps followed by games, finance and news are the most popular categories. The only newspaper mobile addicts see is on their phone. The only bank branch they visit is the one in their pocket.

To succeed, an app has to offer immediate utility, convenience, value and ease of use. Users must feel that an app benefits their lives. They don't want to be marketed to, but they are eager to get information that is timely, personal and relevant. Consumers increasingly expect to have everything they need in their pocket.

Smartphones and apps have become a part of everyone's life. The newest apps featuring simple, easy-to-use interfaces on top of complex tasks are setting and re-setting new standards every day. App interoperability (e.g. Outlook opens and accesses LinkedIn) and apps that leverage the native functions of smartphones and tablets (think GPS) are shaping consumers' perceptions of app value and utility. If you've used Uber or Amazon Prime you will no longer tolerate long load times, broken graphics, hard-to-find buttons, inoperative links or other common technical hiccups.

Simple segments appear to be emerging:

iOS vs Android. iPhone users are slightly more upscale and older. The median iPhone user earns 40 percent more than the median Android user. They use their smartphones nine hours more each month than Android users, reflecting a general pattern among younger users.

Gender. Men dominate travel, transportation and sports apps. Women lead the way in using photo and video sharing apps, weather, games, fitness and health and social media apps. Women are more likely to access mobile coupons while men tend to do price comparisons on mobile devices.

Time of Day. Morning app use focuses on news, weather and travel. Daytime sees spikes in music, business and finance. Peak social time falls after dinner between 8 and 9 pm. Late night seems to have a "me time" component where apps for media, gaming, entertainment and social networks get some play.

Given these stats and emerging patterns, savvy marketers are thinking hard about the value of a virtual private network (VPN) in the pockets of millions of brand fans or followers with the potential to become advocates. Creating a branded app that meets the relevance, speed, utility and convenience criteria isn't easy.

But if you can finesse the technical, data and political issues, you will enable your brand to directly message consumers, craft alerts, publish geo-centric or personalized push notifications, gather immediate feedback and input, collect consumer data, enable couponing or commerce and have an always-on connection to customers. The key to success is knowing your customer base, leveraging your existing technology infrastructure and planning for consumers' next moves.

5 Ways to Test Mobile Advertising

Surprisingly more brands than you think have yet to get into mobile media or advertising. The prudent professionally paranoid marketer will get started and become smarter about mobile media and marketing now. During the ascent phase, prices are affordable. Content and merchant partners are flexible and open to experimentation. And so far, nobody, with the possible exception of Facebook, has a lock on a killer app, game-changing technology or critical market segments.

Here are 5 tips to get started in framing your own mobile marketing program.

Focus on Core Values. Lead with your long suit. Don't try everything at once. Try one thing. Buy display, mobile search or in-app ads promoting the product or service most in-demand by your customers or prospects. Zero-in on something closely identified with your brand identity or your unique selling proposition.

Solicit Response. Ask customers to do one thing. Ask them to choose, vote, sign up, get a coupon, set an alert, watch a video or take an exclusive offer. Validate the reach and acceptability of this channel and test your ability to influence incremental changes in behavior. Get them one thing they can do, easily and quickly. If they like it, this will add to their warm and fuzzy feelings about your brand.

Cross Platforms. Mobile gives marketers a tool to act or react in real time and to influence on-the-go behavior. A positive mobile interaction expands and rounds out the brand experience. Use mobile to get customers to respond to breaking news or a trending social topic. Given the huge percent of email opened on mobile devices, make an offer that is text-response only; or, solicit a vote, a review or opinions about something they see or hear in another media channel. This is an opportunity to jump on a social meme, skate on a big event or associate your brand with something going on in the news or in popular culture that will show your core customers that you get it.

Make an Offer. In return for taking a mobile action within a fixed time frame, customers should get a reward. Rewards can take the form of contest entries, discounts, freebies or coupons and exclusive access to people, places or things. Mobile media is a direct response platform. Stimulate the response, begin to capture opt-ins, look for inflection points like time, geography or life stage where your brand will be easily welcomed.

Ask for Feedback. Do a customer satisfaction or post-purchase survey using mobile media to gauge customer reactions and gather customer input and feedback. Consumers expect short, fast two-way conversations using text messaging or apps. Meet their expectations. Mobile marketing is evolving. Who better to help you plan step number two than the folks who responded to your initial foray?

Mobile Coupons on the March

If you think only little old ladies clip and use coupons, think again. Coupons have gone mobile– big time—both in numbers and in their impact on shopping decisions.

Smartphones have become coupon-finding radars for many consumers. Forty nine percent of consumers surveyed used their smartphones to receive coupons, while roughly 40 percent will redeem a mobile coupon this year. Invesp believes that 8 in 10 consumers will be using mobile coupons this year; half will seek them out while in the store. But widespread usage is just part of the story.

More than half of shoppers, in the Valassis 2016 Purse String Survey, report visiting a store after receiving a coupon on their mobile device. Seven in ten have used their smartphones to find a coupon while they are in the store. Eight in ten non-grocery shoppers use their phones to find coupons before they head out to the mall. A third look specifically for coupons on the same day prior to a store visit.

The average shopper (4 in 10) has installed or used two or fewer coupon apps. Favorites seem to be split evenly between specific sites and general discounters (e.g. Amazon or Groupon) and coupon-specific apps like SnipSnap, Coupons.com or Coupon Sherpa. Increasingly, consumers are rallying to apps that aggregate deals and to grocery apps that automatically find and apply discounts to frequently purchased items. Not only are mobile coupons a factor in deciding when and where to shop; they also impact shopping volume and behavior.

Almost six in every ten shoppers redeem a coupon digitally. Sixty five percent of customers redeemed a mobile coupon within 5 minutes of receipt; many of these were messages triggered by proximity or geo-fencing. One in four consumers increased their basket size when using mobile coupons. Seventy-seven percent spend $10-$50 more than anticipated when redeeming mobile coupons and 39 percent spend more if they receive a personalized coupon.

Coming soon are more, easier-to-use mobile coupons, which will rely on built-in electronic interactions between smartphones, apps, mobile wallets and POS systems.

Here are 3 tips to ensure your success in using online coupons:

Be Clear and Simple. Online shoppers scan. They don't read. Make the offer BIG and bold. Be sure it's fat finger friendly. Make the time frame easy to see. Specify qualifications, shipping costs and whether the offer can be combined with others. Put the terms and conditions upfront in big type.

Go Low Involvement. Don't make customers download software to print coupons. Offer PDFs and simple ways to print or store the coupon quickly. The more time lapsed, the less likelihood of redemption.

Do the Backend First. Don't even begin the coupon game until you've road- tested the underlying technology. Make sure that POS, credit card processing, shopping carts and accounting systems can accept, process and fulfill their wishes.

Mobile couponing is ascendant and closely related to the acceptance and growth of mobile wallets. Savings, security and convenience drive adoption. Brands need to adopt a Do it For Me (DiFM) mantra combined with data to improve personalization, utility and relevance to customers or segments when designing mobile coupon programs.

4 Ways to Use SMS as a Brand Asset

SMS is becoming a commercial channel for brands. Consumers' widespread use of text messaging is making room for select brands to communicate directly with those who opt in.

As 80 percent of US online adults use smartphones, these wireless devices, in the words of Facebook's Margaret Gould Stewart, "have assumed a central position in everyday life...as hyper-personalized, multipurpose power tools...right inside our pockets." New psychological research found that "feelings for brands are much like feelings for friends." Using this data, married to use patterns, offers openings for brands to gain 24/7mobile access to key audiences.

With the average user checking their smartphone 60 times each day or once every 17 minutes, there is a great opportunity for brands to earn their way into the hearts, minds and screens of best customers. Eighty percent of consumers find SMS less intrusive and easier to use than apps. Add to that insight from Teradata indicating that 94 percent of SMS messages are opened within 3 minutes and that 98 percent of the text is read, which is three times more that tweets and 4 times more than email. SMS is immediate, personal, intimate, psychological and responsive, channel qualities that marketers crave.

The trick to building SMS into brand asset requires 4 critical moves.

Drive Opt-Ins. Ask your customers or prospects for permission to text them. Offer up SMS as an additional service. Give them a good immediate reason or an incentive to sign up. Understand that only a small segment, probably a younger millennial one, will act at this time.

Focus on permission for notifications of new merchandise, sales, deals and rewards, since a recent study from Retale says that 89 percent of millennials are likely to respond to notifications from their favorite brands. Push notifications are a springboard step in building brand loyalty. According to Kahuna Research, the average long and short-term retention rates for users who have opted in for push notifications is more than twice as high for those who haven't.

Be Relentlessly Relevant. Only send SMS messages that people will really care about. Edit yourself. Protect the immediacy or privacy of this channel by only sending information, offers or notifications that your customers are very likely to care about. Factor in time of day and day of week to be sure that your SMS communications are relevant at an exact moment in time. Use personal, purchase or behavioral data to decide what to send and when. SMS access is a rare gift, which must not be overused or abused with SPAM.

Think Local. 94 percent of millennials use location-based services. Geo-location apps and notifications are becoming increasingly commonplace and reasonably well accepted. Proximity and immediacy should drive your strategy. Selectively and carefully offer SMS messages that can be instantly scanned and instantly understood as valuable (deals, offers, coupons, specials, exclusives). Limit availability by time to drive more engagement or action and to validate the channel's utility.

Converse. SMS is a two-way conversation. Anticipate the ebb and flow of the conversation your brand wants to have and develop your program accordingly. People text back and forth routinely. They expect an exchange of texts and an opportunity to interact. Plan for one that rewards the consumer and enhances the brand experience.

The Secret of Pokémon Go's Success

The out-of-the blue success of Pokémon Go is a testament to smart strategy and strong execution of a mobile-first campaign. With average play time of 43 minutes, Pokémon Go instantly broke into the top usage tier of apps beating WhatsApp and Facebook Messenger.

Many brands will try to copy the formula to activate a customer base or grab a headline. Here's how they did it.

Start with a known. Pokémon has been around for 20 years in multiple channels. There's hardly a family that hasn't seen a Pokemon TV show or movie, or doesn't have a plush toy or action figure. Leveraging the familiar, tapping into nostalgia, and trading on established affinity jump-starts the program.

Leverage behavior. Gaming and smartphones go together like peanut butter and jelly. By using embedded technology in a new way, the campaign mixed new and familiar behavior so finding players was easy. The same holds true for the share-ability of the experience. Lots of people could access the app and they were quick to tell their friends and family.

Focus on Game Play. Pokémon Go is a classic use of game play and game mechanics. It gives users a choice of teams, puts them into competition to collect objects, rewards them with points and challenges them with increasingly scarce and difficult tasks. These are fundamental elements of virtually every successful game. The planners made sure anyone could play by using intuitive and familiar mechanics.

Fun and Familiar. Pokémon Go is light-hearted and instinctively fun. The combination of online and offline experience, linked to a local geography and local trivia, add excitement and tidbits of local interest. The experience plays on emotion and empowers players to enjoy a regular activity in a new and stimulating way.

The secret of Pokémon Go's success is thoughtful game design tied to smart strategic marketing. The AR technology is not particularly cutting edge, but the thinking behind this marketing phenomenon is.

SECTION VI

SOCIAL MEDIA

Does Social Media Work?

As we embrace, understand and utilize social media as a channel, we have to recognize that thirteen years after Facebook came onto the scene, hype and wishful thinking are far ahead of the measurable reality. Social media adoption is a near universal act of faith. But whether social media works to definitively deliver brand awareness, preference, sales or loyalty is still up for debate, as is the role of social media in a marketing or media mix.

This is the observation of the intellectual property lawyers at Morrison & Foerster, authors of the Socially Aware blog. According to partner John Delaney, "There's a lot of turmoil and uncertainty right now around social media marketing. Although companies continue to spend more money on this channel as consumers increasingly rely on social media for their information, many of them are still trying to figure out best in class strategies and measurements."

Citing stats on dramatically increased spending on social media and the infrastructure to support it, Mr. Delaney sees a mismatch between inputs and outputs. "Companies continue to increase their social media spend, they do not do a particularly good job at engaging customers through social media, and they still struggle to determine the return on investment."

There are limitations and challenges inherent in harnessing or mobilizing social media to suit brand objectives. Although American B-to-C brands have embraced an average of seven social platforms, measurement, sales impact and customer and loyalty are still largely unknown.

Why? Consider these 5 unspoken truths.

Blizzard of Blah-Blah. There is a lot crap in social media. The prescient philosophers, pundits, prophets and prognosticators are outnumbered 100 to 1 by people sharing ordinary, banal and off color thoughts. And while user-generated content (UGC) has become venerated, it's more of an indicator that people want to speak up and participate than it is a rich source of information or insight. Social media is talk radio. A vocal minority drives the conversation while the majority watches and listens voyeuristically.

No Measurement Standard. Marketers don't agree on what or how to measure the business impact of social media. We are eager to "engage," though everyone has a different definition of the term and a different rationale for using it. So we count unique visitors and clicks. We track page views and time spent. We collect repeat visits, opt-ins, submissions and reviews. We are testing new tools to follow users through the sales funnel. But we can't clearly or definitively attribute purchases, beyond self-reported surveys, to social media and compare them with the fixed and variable costs of entry to establish believable or scalable ROI calculations.

Voice and Content Isn't Easy. Brands confront challenges in finding their voice and discerning a point of entry into the conversation. Do you leap into the conversation or ease your way in quietly? Do you wait to be introduced or do you push your way in? Do you act on your own agenda or do you follow the threads you find?

Brands have a posture and a sensibility that shapes the way they communicate. Content is momentarily king, although many brands struggle with what to say, how to say it, how often and to whom. And while anyone can throw up a Facebook page or open a Twitter account, hitting the right tone, the right frequency and the right content is not a slam-dunk.

Labor Intensity. Somebody has to monitor the channels, devise the content, coordinate the offers, measure the traffic, gauge the sentiment, identify the openings, assess the competitive landscape, keep on top of technical developments, check with the lawyers and align the whole shebang with the business objectives of the brand. This takes lots of people.

No Tactical Consensus. Social media could be a marketer's Swiss Army knife: part reach medium, part frequency extender, part direct marketing tool, part coupon distributor, part early warning radar, part intelligence gathering tool, part press release distributor and part promotion platform. We know it's big, but we don't quite know what to do with or how to use it for optimum effect in spite of increasingly sophisticated pitches from the social networks.

So we experiment, test-and-learn, tout all kinds of metrics and convince our bosses to keep playing around with social media 'til we hit on something that makes a difference. Anyone who tells you otherwise is kidding him or herself. Seeing the speed bumps allows us to fit social media into an integrated marketing tool set that powers and grows brands. At the moment, the lawyers are right. The jury is still out.

Using Social Media for B2B Impact

Business-to-Business (B2B) marketers are still skeptical about social media. In spite of widespread popular adoption, Facebook, Twitter and others inspire doubt and hesitation. Brands are uncertain if these networks reach their prospects and customers, are unsure of what to say and how to engage using these evolving channels and are unclear about the impact on sales or the ROI.

That's why Brandwatch email produced the B2B Special Media Report; an analysis of 200 US and UK B2B brands assessing multiple channels and more than 5 million online conversations. They found much more action that you'd imagine.

Here are the key takeaways:

B2B Brands Are Using Social Media. 76percent of brands studied own at least one account on Facebook or Twitter. The average Twitter account has 47,023 followers. The average Facebook account has 211,872 likes or fans. Significant conversation also takes place on blogs (2623 times/day), news sites (5055 times/day), forums (2935 times/day) and video or image sites (375 times/day).

The average brand in this study received 104,000 mentions per year. As you might imagine, bigger brands with billions in revenue and tens of thousands of employees have been the early and more effective adopters. IBM is the global standout.

Volume and Impact Vary by Sector. Software manufacturers dominate the social B2B space accounting for 54 percent of overall discussion. Military defense, chemicals and heavy industry are the laggards in terms of social media adoption.

Yet in spite of the volume, the amount of earned media, comments and pass-alongs generated by the software guys is significantly less than the aerospace sector where each post generates an average of 250 downstream mentions. In fact, the more the software firms post, the less earned media they earn. So, it's not how much you post but how it resonates that matters.

Brands Mirror Audiences. The use of language, industry jargon, videos and hashtags on B2B social sites is "strikingly similar" to business audiences. Participants are 65 percent male and 35 percent female. Posts are 54 percent photos, 33 percent links, 10 percent videos and 3 percent text status updates. Status updates drive the smallest number of likes and shares.

Sales Clues Abound. The most commonly discussed topic related to the sales cycle is the price and value of a potential sale; in some sectors it's as much as 60 percent of the conversations. This is a huge opportunity to proactively address questions and objections as well as to gauge the sensibilities of vertical markets.

Customer service is a big topic. Though too many brands do not actively respond to or answer online complaints. Just one percent of 140,000 negative comments were directly addressed by B2B brands. This is a huge miss since addressing complaints, questions and rumors can build brand affinity and spike out potential stumbling blocks to sales. It can also offer ways to differentiate a brand and develop competitive advantage.

Interestingly, the lowest volume but highest value conversations concern purchase intent. Among the 200 brands studied, there were 72,756 expressions of purchase intent in the last year. On average, brands receive 363 potential leads, or one each day. Twenty-three percent come from executives at other firms, a directional measure of lead quality. Addressing just a fraction of these potential leads could result in significant revenue or share growth.

B2B use of social media is still in its infancy. "This latent adoption is an opportunity, rather than a deterrent," according to Brandwatch. Increasingly, business decision-makers are embracing social media and B2B brands should stake their claims and begin to develop engagement and content strategies.

Re-Thinking Facebook

Now that Facebook has eliminated free reach, brands have to rethink and reformulate their Facebook strategies.

Reducing access to followers and fans has turned Facebook from an owned or earned property into paid media. This effectively kills carefully constructed editorial and posting strategies since no one will actually see a post unless it's sponsored. The editorial/advertising one-two punch is over. Staffing teams of content producers and community managers to monitor, post and respond in real time knowing that the content will reach less than 5percent of the fan base is now wasteful.

Brands thinking that they would manage customer service issues, engage customers or showcase different facets of their product, service or company are mostly out of luck. Brands hoping to leverage massive traffic and consumer interaction once provided by Facebook have to decide to either build their own online communities or to ally with other social platforms who have more attractive operating terms.

Brands embraced Facebook because it gave us a window into the hearts, minds and behaviors of our customers. Anxious for any type of interaction, we tested photos, videos, memes, sayings, coupons, promotions and topical observations. That's why Facebook became a cornerstone of social strategy for so many brands. Desperate to get a response from our followers, some of us developed response benchmarks to beat, and tested editorial cadences to drive likes, comments, shares and new followers.

Most of us came to believe that 80 percent of branded posts could be planned with 20 percent left to involve ourselves in ongoing and developing conversations. We stood in awe of infrequent virility, like the Oreo Super Bowl post, which yielded much more in bragging rights for marketers than it did in increments of brand preference or cases of cookies sold.

Since it was cheap, we convinced ourselves, with Facebook's help, that soft measures like "engagement" would be sufficient to assess the value of the platform and justify the investment of time and dollars. We did this knowing that the research showed that 9 out of 10 posts got zero response. And the vast majority of Facebook subscribers are passive users.

We looked the other way as a billion people adopted Facebook as a cross between Reader's Digest and a personal CRM system to keep track of friends and family. We didn't want to believe we were interlopers. We ignored the fact that the average Facebook user really likes those baby pictures, cat videos, check-ins, re-posted news stories, angry responses to current events, vacation videos and news bytes of lifestyle and family activities.

The more we pay, the more we have to track, measure and justify ROI. Facebook's greed offers us a reality check and an opportunity to re-think and recalibrate how we use this social platform, especially for brands without unlimited budgets. Consider these six principles:

Focus on Business Goals. What do we need to achieve and how will Facebook help us get there? Is it sales, shares, new names, loyalty, contest entries, reviews or UGC? Initially, we used social media to expose hidden facets of the brand, flesh out brand character and personality and find common ground with customers and prospects. This is still theoretically possible, but at what CPA? Measuring progress toward business objectives and the cost-per-result is the starting and the ending point.

Plot Facebook in an Ecosystem. If you do eCommerce on the branded website and relationship marketing by email, what role does Facebook play in the grand plan? Is it a device to drive new opt-ins? Is it a mechanism to distribute coupons? Is it a channel for solving customer service issues? Does it play a role in expanding or amplifying a new ad campaign? Being clear about the tasks needed and the outcomes expected should shape your Facebook content and buy.

Pre-Think the Conversation. We know how Facebook works (or doesn't). Start with the predictable interplay of content and customers. Shape the message to drive the intended action. Leverage what worked in the past. Emphasize images over copy. Include a clear call to action. Splurge for Timeline placement. Measure and negotiate everything.

Pick Your Shots. Nobody can afford daily sponsored posts. So brands have to decide which retail calendar events, which seasonal product promotions, which new product introductions or which competitive moves or marketplace trends are worthy of a reaction and a supplemental investment. As Facebook becomes a marketers' slot machine, we have to hedge our bets and reduce the number and quantity of posts in search of fewer, more impactful interactions.

Make Videos. Video is becoming the dominant social and mobile medium. Facebook is gearing up to challenge YouTube and to knock out Vimeo and Hulu. Consumers watch more and longer videos than brands produce. Placing your TV spot on Facebook or YouTube yields much less viewing, sharing and interacting than you think. Make how-to, lifestyle and product or service videos part of your updated Facebook strategy.

Demand Data Sharing. Facebook doesn't share. They'll match their database with yours and then sell you distribution to the names that match. But they won't tell you who on your list is a Facebook subscriber. They'll also use your data for their own purposes. And they get antsy about scraping profile data when consumers log or opt-in using their Facebook sign on to connect with brands. This one-way attitude has to be resisted by brands, especially those spending big bucks. If Facebook really wants to help marketers and brands succeed, then sharing is caring.

Many marketers are still thinking about and planning to use the Facebook of two years ago. Facebook's partnership and sales posture has aggressively evolved, as have their terms of brand engagement. Brands need to meet them head on, recognize and adapt to the changed landscape, reject the take-it or leave-it mentality and remember that we wield the dollars that fuel their burgeoning empire.

Facebook is a Direct Marketing Machine

There is nothing subtle in Facebook's move to curate, qualify and market audience segments. Absent is the long-standing claim that Facebook is strictly about relationships, sharing, engagement and saving the world.

Most of the magic is a three-stage data mining process. By taking data from brands and combining it with demographic, psychographic and behavioral data from third party sources like Epsilon, Acxiom and Datalogix, marketers can get a tighter bead on likely buyers.

Then, by matching combined brand and outside data with Facebook profiles, the platform can deliver a specific message to large numbers of individuals meeting very narrow criteria, eliminating waste and optimizing the likelihood that consumers will opt-in, share, sign-up, download or buy something. Like traditional publishers or broadcasters, Facebook claims to offer seamless and measurable targeting, reach and delivery.

Facebook claims a 50 percent accuracy advantage over the average online campaign. This is the Holy Grail for direct marketers: maximum response with minimal waste across channels at efficient costs. For brands without a direct marketing or CRM infrastructure, Facebook potentially is a plug-and-play solution since brands can potentially find and reach their best customers, find more prospects that look like best customers or create new target segments virtually on the fly. But while Facebook will deliver a branded message to targeted users and tell you what percent of your database are on Facebook, they won't share the details or trade data with brands.

With massive reach and strong frequency, based on the fact that people check their newsfeed as much as fourteen times each day, Facebook is looking to take serious market share away from display advertising, search and email marketing.

The social network's leading mobile posture is a second strong direct response argument. With zillions accessing Facebook every day on smartphones and tablets, a brand can reach their customers and prospects and finesse all the costly, complicated and confusing device, rendering and carrier issues with one partner.

Tight targeting and mobile access, when combined with links to branded websites, pixel tracking for retargeting and internal databases, gives a brand continuous exposure to people who have shown any sign of interest. This is, depending on your perspective, either super-targeting or super-stalking. Either way, research shows that it delivers more, faster response.

It also explains how that pair of shoes you looked at on Zappos follows you around the Internet and appears on your Facebook page. Newsfeed or Timeline units, a 154x154 pixel image and several lines of copy, were created precisely to enable precision targeting and pixel tracking to enable retargeting on Facebook and across the web. Consumers can like, share and comment on FBX ads, so virility is baked in.

My clients using these units are reporting strong cost effective results. And even though many have been extorted into buying ads since Facebook choked off access to the fans they accumulated by manipulating the Edgerank algorithm, the guys paying the bills now can find out how many fans, or followers are actually buying products.

Facebook is aggressively addressing direct marketing fundamentals and focusing on critical ROI concerns. Many of their social network peers are following suit. It will be fascinating to see how and how quickly traditional direct response partners respond. Stay tuned. It's about to get very interesting.

Facebook's Retargeting Platform

Retargeting is a killer app for lead generation and eCommerce. The products that mysteriously follow people around the web no longer freak out consumers. And marketers are reveling in the better than average response and conversion rates.

A study of 215 retargeting campaigns that generated 800 million impressions, produced by AdRoll, not only documents this phenomenon, but indicates that Facebook is becoming a dominant and effective retargeting platform. Their evolving direct response ad units and mobile placements are fertile ground for even greater results. And since mobile ad units are new and underutilized, the CPM costs are 57 percent lower than retargeting in the News Feed.

Marketers are experimenting with several different units in different combinations. The News Feed ads (FBX) on desktops combine a large visual with sufficient space or both sell copy and social elements like comments and sharing. The right hand column is smaller and feels like it's designed for high frequency. And now Facebook will match brand website visitors with Facebook users and serve ads exclusively on the basis of the match. This Website Custom Audience (WCA) play adds incremental targeting and gives marketers more options. Combining Facebook units with standard web retargeting appears to be the arena for marketers to test their way to better results.

The reported results are worth considering...

- CTRs for News Feed desktop are 8.1 times greater and CPC was 24 percent less than standard web retargeting
- News Feed on mobile yields a 9.1 times CTR advantage and 79 percent lower costs per click over standard web targeting
- 1+1+1 = >3. Adding mobile to desktop and general web retargeting produces 53 percent more clicks and 58 percent more conversions—a new formula for added yield

As Facebook continues its evolution into a sophisticated direct response mechanism, retargeting will play an important role. It too will evolve as it becomes more personalized and more carefully triggered.

Using Twitter

Twitter, the 140-character social media network, part news ticker, part party line, part celebrity cage match and part message forwarding service, confounds as many brands.

Its skyrocketing awareness, intense exchanges, time sensitive use patterns and its regular intrusion into the global news cycle keep us guessing about if, how or when to embrace Twitter as a commercial channel. With 350 million unique users a month, Twitter works like talk radio. A minority drives the conversation while a majority watches and listens but don't actively participate. Twitter embodies a basic human voyeuristic curiosity—FOMO. Millions don't want to miss what's happening.

The hashtag convention (#subject), Twitter's unique contribution to social technology and culture, makes it easy to find and participate in any conversation. Hashtags have become a cultural meme; radar blips for monitoring conversations, scouting trends and policing brand reputations. Hashtags make it easy to follow or participate in broad public conversations on a block, neighborhood, local, national or global scale.

Twitter has established seven key roles for itself.

News Ticker. Twitter is a news source, a barometer of reactions to breaking news and a news distribution channel. Twitter is effectively a participatory global news ticker. People routinely tweet eyewitness accounts, videos and images of breaking stories often before traditional news outlets. One in four includes a link to either the original story or to other content that complements, enhances, disputes or counterattacks the topics at hand.

Political Megaphone. Donald Trump has turned Twitter into a must-see version of FDR's radio chats. Twitter gives political activists a way to work around government censorship and a somewhat tamper-proof communications tool to contact and rally followers or supporters. It has become the go-to medium for Presidential candidates and elected officials to punch and counterpunch and for advocates to telegraph their moves, reply to accusations or rally support.

Event Companion. Twitter is a real time side-by-side simultaneous group experience for live, broadcast, streaming or recorded events. Who can forget Oreo's famous "dunk in the dark" Super Bowl tweet, or Ellen DeGeneres' Oscar selfie? On Twitter, participants, viewers and wannabees comment, react, critique, free associate, embellish or add complementary or contradictory information in the moment. Twitter expands the audience and amplifies events.

Research from Canvus suggests that when Twitter users are simultaneously watching TV and see or express strong emotions about the content of a show, ad recall increases. When a high percentage of tweets contain emotional words and reactions, viewers are 40 percent more likely to recall an ad in the show. Those actively monitoring Twitter during a show increased recall by 62 percent and those creating emotional tweets are three times more likely to recall ads. So, in theory, Twitter enhances TV viewing and improves advertising effectiveness.

Celebrity Promotion Platform. Everyone from the Pope to porn stars promote on Twitter. Movies, books, music, theater, TV and gossip are routinely featured alongside celebrity shout outs and slugfests.

Early Warning Radar. Twitter enables brands to assess social sentiment, establish benchmarks, follow or prompt viral transmissions and measure market or message penetration and relevance. Many brands check the impact or resonance of TV commercials or important promotions by looking for reactions on Twitter.

Coupon Distributor. A third of registered Twitter users signed up to get deals and discounts. Brands regularly tweet coupons and discount codes. Others offer sneak previews or limited time and exclusive access to new merchandise or discounted pricing.

Customer Service Channel. Twitter enables real time praise and complaints as well as a channel to address and respond to either. Brands are engaging and monitoring the flow of positive and negative opinion, responding to operational or performance problems, recruiting new personnel and engaging customer issues with credit, shipping, returns and merchandise.

The implications of these seven dominant uses of Twitter are:

Be Prepared. Anticipate the conversations related to your brand. Prepare and pre-clear copy, images, video and links to jump into the fray at the right moment. Twitter moves fast and the complexion of conversations can change in a nanosecond. You have to be ready, have a plan and have a skilled community manager in place.

Monitor the Channel. Monitor conversations and subjects likely to affect your brand or offering a logical opening to associate your brand with an ongoing topic. Know when to hold and when to commit. Sentiment and intensity should guide you. Don't get caught up in the emotion of the moment or get baited into a compromising response.

Pick Your Shots. Understand what conversations your brand can reasonably connect to. Stay close to how consumers have sorted or perceived your brand. Your tweets must be relevant in the moment and reflect the sensibilities of the people following it. This requires advance rules of engagement and clear guidelines on language, attitude and brand posture. It's easy to get dragged into an uncomfortable rant, to draw big volumes of negative and pile-on attention or to be perceived as flat-footed and out of it.

Twitter empowers brands to harness immediacy, connectivity and the sharing instinct. It encourages brands to find and engage active talkers and sharers in service to brand awareness, preference and purchase intent. Brands need to understand the channel and allocate time and resources to optimize Twitter's value.

Tumblr Tumbles into Adland

Now that they've drawn a crowd, Tumblr is still trying to figure out how to make a buck. They've marshaled traffic, usage and psycho-demographic stats and are trying to simultaneously associate themselves with Facebook, Twitter and Pinterest to gain consideration and access to social ad budgets, while differentiating themselves from the competition to attract specific brands and buys.

To do this, Tumblr raises a couple of new ideas about the use and value of social networks for brands.

Play the Platform. Tumblr argues that they are a two-fer—an independent web platform featuring an easy to use CMS, which can fit seamlessly into a brand's overall digital ecosystem, and a large and growing global social network. Creating a branded Tumblr, marketers can expand reach, add link juice and add to a robust content strategy by creating a digital brand asset.

A blank canvas, a Tumblr blog can be anything, though the more successful ones are highly visual, featuring striking images, videos and gifs. There are no comment options, beyond reblogging, so sentiment tends to be more positive than on other social platforms.

A branded Tumblr page is part of the Tumblr network and its emerging topical community subsets. This potentially yields some endorsement by association and the prospect of added viral distribution, not to mention a future ad targeting option.

Free Virility. In contrast to Facebook, who has choked off access to followers, Tumblr argues that reblogging is an engine of goodness for brands. Each individual blogger creates a Tumblr post, which is often curated and reblogged by others who reach large audiences, where reblogging takes place again. They have created a waterfall chart to help marketers wrap their heads around this fundamental social media concept. The only missing part is hard data to prove it.

One uniquely interesting aspect of Tumblr reblogging is a latency period. More than half of reblogs take place more than 15 days after an original post. This suggests either that usage is less frequent or intense or that users take their time and give more consideration to the memes they share.

But in spite of these interesting sales pitches, buying Tumblr is a challenge. Blog content is highly visual and idiosyncratic. Users only see content from those they follow. To develop significant followings to get substantial reach and/or frequency against desirable segments, brands will have to accumulate followers. Brands need to know why people use Tumblr and how the people and their intentions, moods and behaviors differ from the other social networks.

You can follow anyone without his or her blessing, so the WOM value and personal endorsement aspect is likely to be weaker than on Facebook. Each user follows a different set of bloggers and nobody has crunched the numbers to determine what the patterns and affinities might be, so aggregating audiences at scale is not really possible.

Content categories aren't marketing channels. So far, targeting options are limited to gender and geography—hardly sophisticated tools. For example, Tumblr attracts 12.8 million moms (referred to as Mumblrs) but there is no clear or easy path to reach them!

Tumblr has a sizeable audience, but they haven't yet packaged it to sell to advertisers. Maybe this reflects tension between the original intention of founder David Karp and the aggressive plans of acquirer Marissa Mayer. But unless they get much more serious about slicing and dicing the audience and giving marketers a reason to buy, they will not be competitive.

5 Ways to Optimize Instagram

Instagram, the photo and video-sharing app owned by Facebook, has become a serious player in a very short time. Instagram has 300 million unique monthly users spending 21 minutes per month uploading 70 million images each day with 2.5 billion likes in any given 24 hour period.

Twenty percent of all Internet users and 77 million Americans, or 27.6 percent of the US population, access the network. Thirty percent of the traffic is in the United States where 49 percent of registered adults use the app every day, almost half on a smartphone.

According to research by L2, Instagram registers 15 times the engagement and double the engaged user base of its parent, Facebook, and has surpassed Twitter in both volume and intensity of customer engagement. Socialbakers, focusing on the top 25 most engaging brands on Instagram, found that the average rate of engagement per post on Instagram was almost 5 times greater than a post on Twitter.

Instagram has become the preferred social platform for US teens and for substantial numbers of young adults. More than 56 percent of US Internet users, 14-17, have Instagram accounts. So do 41 percent of Internet users 16-24. Thirty-two percent of US teens say Instagram is their favorite social network.

Unlike its parent, for the moment, Instagram offers brands 100 percent organic, viral access to their fans, though observers expect that this free reach will be curtailed in order to drive ad revenues. With a 94 percent usage overlap with Facebook and connected back-end pipes, Instagram usage data is merged with its parent, can use Facebook's segmented and sophisticated standing or customized targeting channels.

Many brands have experimented with presenting ads on one platform and retargeting on the other. One study found that ads on Instagram had recall 2.8 times higher than the average online ad. Mercedes Benz publicly reported a 54 percent increase in website visits when advertising on both networks in tandem.

Instagram created ad units, including a video feature, revamped its carousel and shortly will enable brands to issue a call to action (CTA). Also in the works is an effort to develop infrastructure to support sign-ups, opt-ins, downloads, direct purchasing and other forms of lead generation. The ability to sponsor and target content on this network will make Instagram an even more potent advertising channel.

Given the visual nature of this social network and its engagement potential, consider these five tactics to get your fair share of Instagram attention, sharing and love.

Intercept Behavior. Post at least once a week. Assume most users will see your post on a smartphone or tablet. Construct images and manage sizing appropriately. Post at times when users are likely to pay attention. Think about commuting times, lunchtime, after dinner and other moments during the day that people crave diversion, surprise and entertainment. Instagram is perceived as an authentic collection of ideas and images, curated by trusted sources. There might not be a better synthesis of targeting, content and channels.

Sell by Showing. Photos and fifteen second videos are the coin of the realm. Don't be afraid to stump your users by posting something unusual or unexpected. Similarly, images of good-looking people, celebrities, oddities, behind-the-scenes activities, images with different tones, perspectives or coloration will get enough attention to be shared. Instagram might be the absolute proof that a picture is worth a thousand words. Pictures often communicate fundamental ideas and emotions without a need for translation.

Facilitate Sharing. Comments, re-posts and sharing to other social networks, especially Facebook (9 out of 10 shares) and Twitter, are common. Instagram, like Twitter, is becoming a real-time companion to off-line events.

Use Hashtags (#) to be Found. Eight-six percent of brands on the platform use them. Participate in the ongoing conversations or trends by using the @mentions convention. Posts that mention other users average 37 percent higher engagement, probably because there is a widespread understanding and expectation that friends share interests, tastes, perspectives and Instagram imagery.

Captions Count. Craft punchy captions that complement the image. Worry less about length than about how the words reflect or amplify the images. Funny, ironic, off-beat, startling or unexpected captions work best. Tag locations. Posts with locations garner 50 percent more engagement than those without.

Use Your Ecosystem. Import Instagram images and user-generated content into branded websites and Facebook pages. Many brands run contests either to create, comment on or curate images. Instagram integration adds an element of real-time spontaneity that feels natural and comfortable to consumers.

Instagram offers brands a different angle of attack to consumers. With its built-in connection to Facebook and evolving approach to brands and advertising, it can become an important tool in your marketing arsenal.

Using YouTube to the Max

Everybody knows that YouTube is the second most used search engine. Everybody knows that YouTube is SEO optimized. And everybody knows that more than one billion unique visitors watch more than four billion hours of video on YouTube each month. That's why 100 of the top 100 advertisers post videos and create channels on YouTube.

But did you know that most brands post videos without much of a strategy and hope for the best? Or did you know that many brands post videos that don't match the interests or viewing patterns of their most likely customers or prospects?

That's the insight Pixabilty brings to the table in measuring and analyzing YouTube as a communications platform. Their study analyzed 18.9 billion CE views on 113,780 specialized CE channels, turned up these ten expected and not-so-expected observations:

Brands are Minority Publishers. Only 23 percent of CE views are attributable to brands. Three-quarters of the videos about phones, tablets, computers, cameras, wearables, etc. come from other sources, some of which have significantly more credibility and share-ability than the leading brands.

Viewing influences purchases. Videos about tablets and smartphones prompt more than 334 million views per month. Forty-eight 48percent of tablet buyers and 61 percent of smartphone buyers watched a video on YouTube before they bought.

TV Spots Don't Play. Branded TV commercials represent 37 percent of all CE videos. It's standard operating procedure, a free reach extender, to put a spot on the brand's YouTube channel. But the fact that they only pull 10 percent of the views indicates their relative ineffectiveness in the social sphere.

Length Matters. Brands produce short videos, generally no more than three minutes in duration. But viewers watch more than twice as many videos that run eight to 10 minutes in length. There is an appetite for extended storytelling that's being underserved.

More is Not Better. Frequent posting doesn't seem to guarantee attention. Seventy-five percent of all CE videos on YouTube get less than 10,000 viewers. Don't be seduced by the fact that there are 325 channels with a million or more subscribers. Most videos on YouTube go relatively unnoticed. The burden is to develop content that resonates with consumers because it entertains, distracts, informs or intrigues.

Celebrity Counts. Branded videos featuring celebrities and elaborate storylines attract 123X as many views as the average CE video. Developing unique online video seems to be the formula for penetrating consumers' consciousness.

Different Topics Play Differently. Product teasers are the most popular CE content on YouTube drawing 21 percent of engagement from just 12 percent of all videos. Videos testing the limits of products or showing head-to-head product comparisons account for more than half of all engagement in the category. Surprisingly, spoofs, how-to's, celebrity endorsements and expert interviews collectively only account for 12 percent of CE videos.

Timing Plays a Role. Consumers turn to brand videos and teasers before products launch or reach the market. But after a new product hits the market, vloggers and user generated videos rule. Audiences seem to appreciate the often entertaining and somewhat independent voices of peer content creators.

Optimization is Crucial. Too many publishers skimp on keywords and tagging. The top 25 percent brands use 1/5X more metadata tags than the bottom 25 percent. Similarly, the leading brands use 8X more playlists to differentiate and sort videos making them easier to find.

Search behavior spikes around product launches, not around the traditional retail calendar. Many brands focus enhanced search efforts or amp up paid search or sponsored videos on President's Day or Black Friday, rather than zero- in on the days surrounding a global product introduction.

Be Directive. Viewers are seeking answers and information. Brands that ask for social sharing and drive viewers to registration pages using conversion links and art cards at the end of videos get considerable compliance. Brands using conversion links effectively drive almost double the desired interactions with consumers.

YouTube has evolved from a default repository of video into a series of multi-dimensional channels that can be measured and benchmarked to help marketers target, reach and persuade consumers. Using this data and observed behavior to inform and improve creative development, reach and frequency optimization, timing and placement feels like a no-brainer.

WHAT'S NEXT?

Predicting the future in a constantly changing digital arena is never easy. But seven trends in the digital marketing universe will shape our thinking in the near term.

Intense Customer Focus. Marketers will intensify their focus on consumer expectations, real-time behavior and the customer journey. Automated efforts will make it easier to track movement through time and space and gather all relevant personal data, from multiple sources, into a robust "golden record." This robust individual profile will be updated regularly and used to anticipate and align with consumers' dominant attitude: what's-in-it-for-me (WiiFM) and their desire for brands to do-it-for-me (DiFM).

Predictive analytics, the data science used to sort, filter, segment or score profiles, will play a role in identity resolution and help to determine optimal inflection points and opportunities to engage customers and prospects on their own terms. Success criteria for consumer interactions and messaging, and for the value of predictive analytics, will be the degree of personal relevance, utility and value delivered to individual consumers.

Privacy & Personalization. There is no privacy. Individuals routinely trade personal information in return for access, deals, discounts and information. Aggregators collect and traffic mountains of psychographic, behavioral, attitudinal, purchase and usage data about everyone. Marketers need to focus on this critical value exchange. There is an often unarticulated quid-pro-quo understanding that to the extent brands "know" their customers, customers expect them to use that information to super-serve them.

Customers are saying, "If you really know me, send me information about the things I care about. Save me time and money. Show me your best stuff first. Make my brand experience easy and fun. Don't waste my time, bomb me with irrelevant messages or ignore me."

Data and Analytics Explosion. Six billion active connected devices churn out 2.5 quintillion bytes of data every day. The explosive growth of mobile devices, social media and messaging apps use robot assistants like Siri or Alexa, and the Internet of Things (IoT) will drive these numbers skyward. Meanwhile, the technology to process this data will get faster and cheaper. Sophisticated predictive analytics, leveraging artificial intelligence (AI), machine learning (ML) and deep learning, or neural network algorithms, will be broadly deployed and used to trigger real-time interactions. In the not-too-distant future, brands will seamlessly and automatically access personal data at the point of sale, on mobile devices, in social networks and online to create hyper-personalized one-to-one experiences.

We are rapidly approaching the one-to-one application of omnichannel data depicted in the Star Trek series or in the 2002 Steven Spielberg film *Minority Report*. Cognitive or behavior-based marketing will extend to automated chatbots, which approximate human interactions in managing a range of tasks. Look for AdTech and MarTech, the leading tech platforms for data processing and ad deployment, to come together, either in mergers or alliances. And watch Oracle, Salesforce, Adobe, IBM and others stitch these technologies together and jockey for market share and position.

Smartphones Rule. Smartphones have become indispensable tools. Apps are evolving into three tiers: daily use, (generally 7-8 per person), utility apps for instant reference or occasional use (e.g. banking, travel or health and wellness), and transitional apps selected and frequently used once, ignored or deleted after use. New apps will add monitoring and alerts functionality, improve on-the-go-messaging, expand video access and quality, introduce more sophisticated games, be used more frequently as virtual private networks (VPNs) and connect the native functionalities built into phones to each other.

Apps will continue to be hit or miss propositions. Marketers must stimulate initial download prompt continuous usage and build deeper relationships with users to remain on the phones. This is an intensely competitive arena, which will morph as phone technology and consumers' phone habits evolve.

Video is Imperative. Video has captured our attention, our imagination and increasing amounts of our time. Video has become ubiquitous online, in social networks and on mobile devices. Seventy-eight percent of online Americans, representing three-quarters of all Internet traffic and between one-third and one-half of all mobile traffic (roughly 147 to 151 million individuals), view videos each month. The average American watches 32 videos each month or one a day. This number soars for teenagers and young adults.

Greater Wi-Fi penetration, bigger data plans from cellular carriers, more advanced compression, better screen resolution plus faster streaming are driving the explosive growth of video consumption. Availability of high quality video cameras on smartphones and simple editing apps have altered what consumers expect from video and have encouraged the amateur filmmakers among us.

Social Media Saturation. Key social networks are maxing out on absolute growth so the battle shifts from acquiring new members to expanding member engagement and uptake of new services. Networks will compete with each other for content consumption and to dominate popular interests like dating, shopping, entertainment and job hunting.

In the interim, Jeff Bezos at Amazon and Mark Zuckerberg at Facebook will vie for world dominance in their respective spheres. Bezos seeks to be the ultimate global merchant while Zuckerberg, according to his latest manifesto, wants to bring the world together to foster meaningful communities and broad scale social, economic, political or religious action within his walled garden.

Evolving Technologies. Artificial Reality (AR) and Virtual Reality (VR) are on the horizon, gated mostly by the availability of content and cost of equipment, which will decline over time. Look for VR arcades and adoption by travel, ecological and medical sectors where this technology can have dramatic educational and persuasive results. Soon, these innovations will have a dramatic impact on creative possibilities and will, over time, set new standards for design and storytelling. My hunch is that widespread consumer adoption will follow changes in device size and weight, processing speed and affordability driven by breakthrough applications in porn or sports.

Similarly, wearables will offer a wide range of opportunities to monitor and report health, fitness and wellness data. Expect a lot of hyped product introductions and hit-or-miss consumer response. Wearables will take off when the novelty wears off and the practical value is broadly established. Eventually, data derived from these emerging technologies will be automatically shared with healthcare professionals, influence pharmaceutical choices and dosing, and will be benchmarked against relevant populations in real time to influence preventive medical treatments. The Fitbit crowd will be early adopters and evangelists. The rest of us will wait and see.

The most productive approach for dancing through the next phases of the digital revolution is to be hard-nosed about meeting business objectives and to be open to the possibilities. Take a test-and-learn attitude toward new options. Don't be afraid to dabble and fail. Agility, flexibility, clear key performance indicators (KPIs) and a healthy risk appetite will separate the winners from the also-rans.

Go forth and experiment!

ACRONYM GLOSSARY

AdTech	Automated Media Tools
AI	Artificial Intelligence
API	Application Program Interface
AR	Augmented Reality
B2B	Business-to-Business
B2C	Business-to-Consumer
B2G	Business-to-Government
BI	Business Intelligence (software)
BOGO	Buy One; Get One
Can SPAM	Anti-SPAM legislation
CDMA	Code Division Multiple Access (Mobile standard)
CDO	Chief Digital Officer
CE	Consumer Electronics
CMS	Content Management System
CPG	Consumer Packaged Goods
CPM	Cost per Thousand

CRM	Customer Relationship Management
CTA	Call-to-Action
CTR	Click Through Rate
CX	Customer Experience
DIY	Do It Yourself
DiFM	Do it For Me
DMP	Data Management Platform
DM	Direct Mail or Direct Marketing
DSP	Demand Side Platform
eM	Email
ESP	Email Service Provider
FOMO	Fear of Missing Out
GPS	Global Positioning System
IAB	Internet Advertising Bureau
IMEI	International Mobile Equipment Identity
KPI	Key Performance Indicators
LTV	Lifetime Value
MAP	Marketing Automation Platform
MarTech	Marketing technology tools
MCM	Multi-Channel Marketing
MDB	Marketing Database
MEID	Mobile Equipment Identifier
MRM	Marketing Resource Management

NPS	Net Promoter Score
NPV	Net Present Value
NRF	National Retail Federation
OS	Operating System
POS	Point of Sale
RFID	Radio Frequency Identification tags
RFM	Recency, Frequency & Monetary Value
ROI	Return on Investment
SDK	Software Development Kits
SEO	Search Engine Optimization (natural search)
SEM	Search Engine Marketing (paid search)
SERP	Search Engine Results Page
SIM	Subscriber Identification Module (mobile phone unique ID)
SLA	Service Level Agreement
SMS	Short Message Service (text messages)
SSP	Supply Side Platform
SUBJ	Email Subject Line
TCO	Total Cost of Ownership
UGC	User Generated Content
URL	Universal Resource Locator (internet address)
UX	User Experience
UXD	User Experience Design
VOC	Voice of the Customer

VIP	Very Important Person
VPN	Virtual Private Network
VR	Virtual Reality
WiFi	Wireless Area Network
WiiFM	What's in it For Me
WOM	Word of Mouth

ABOUT THE AUTHOR

Danny Flamberg is a veteran marketing and advertising strategist and practitioner working with leading, insurgent and start-up brands in the US, Canada, Europe, South America, Asia and the Middle East. An early digital pioneer, he has been blogging as ***The Manhattan Marketing Maven*** since the early days of the digital revolution in the late 1990s building a reputation and following as a digital thinker, innovator and strategist.

A principal and Omni Channel Marketing Leader at Opera Solutions, he has been EVP Managing Director at Publicis, Vice President of Global Marketing at SAP, Senior Vice President and Managing Director at Digitas and CMO of CellularOne, and 1-800-Mattress.

With extensive experience designing direct consumer engagements, CRM acquisition and retention campaigns, loyalty programs and using Big Data to predict and model behavior, he has created measurable income and incremental value for many clients. Danny has worked in almost every industry developing tactical innovations and pioneering strategies for online media and database, mobile and social media marketing.

He earned an A.B, an M.A. and a Ph.D. in econometrics at Columbia University.

Danny lives on Manhattan's Upper West Side.

Made in the USA
Monee, IL
13 September 2026

62981009R00089